THE

GOAN

RHAPSODY

The Identity Crisis That Is Being Goan

ROHIT PINTO

Published by Hemingway Publishers

Cover design by Hemingway Publishers

ISBN: Printed in the United States

Table of Contents

Foreword

"My Goa, my Goa, my wonderful Goa, the beaches are beautiful in Goa; the lights of Marmagoa..." It's a song my father used to sing. I don't know if it's a professional song or one my father made up, but I couldn't find any evidence of it online. It's one of those things I remember from when I was a child. My mother would always sing a different song, Calcutta by The Four Preps (lyrics by Paul Vance and Lee Pockriss), which goes,

"I've kissed the girls in Naples, they're pretty as can be,

I've also kissed some French girls who came from Paris.

The Spanish girls are lovely, oh yes, indeed they are,

But the ladies of Calcutta are sweeter by far.

The ladies of Calcutta will steal your heart away,

And after it is stolen, you'll say,

I've kissed the girls of Naples, I've kissed them in Paris,

But the ladies of Calcutta do something to me."

You see, I'm a product of a marriage between a Goan raised in Goa and Bombay (now Mumbai), and a lady of Goan origin raised in the city of Calcutta (now Kolkata). While both my parents had different experiences, somehow, they both loved the culture and traditions of Goa.

This book is my experience and memories of Goa. It's about a time in Goa that I remember and loved. A time when life was hard and simple, and community was everything. Now things are different. Not better, not worse, just different. As a human, I like to think that I embrace change. But like everyone else, I've been dragged kicking and screaming into the future, which has me looking back to "the good old days".

I've also included stories, some told to me by my grandmother, some by my granduncles, and some others by my parents. I was lucky enough to be the first of my generation on my dad's side, and second on my mom's side (by a little less than a month), so I got to hear a lot of the stories and experiences of the previous generations. As we grew older and the family grew more prosperous, we lost some of the old ways.

This book is not a history lesson. Many have had a different upbringing from the one I had, and hence may not have the same stories or routines. This is my story, my opinions and my recipes. Some may disagree, and that's their prerogative. I ask that you simply enjoy the stories and the recipes for what they are.

PART 1:
MY GOA

Chapter 1: Authenticity is an Illusion

The word "authentic" has little real meaning in the world of food. It doesn't matter what country, village, or town you come from; the name of a dish is just a broad guideline, a suggestion, if you will, of what it might contain or taste like.

Take two families who have lived in the same town for the same number of years or even generations, and ask them to cook the same dish. You'll undoubtedly have two different methods of preparation and two different sets of flavours, both, if you're lucky, delicious. It's like Shakespeare said, "A rose comes in many fragrances, sizes and shapes, but it still smells as sweet". Okay, before the literature purists jump on my case, Shakespeare didn't exactly say that. But "a rose by any other name would smell as sweet," and the point still stands.

The best cooks, in my opinion, are the ones who customize and adapt, which makes every parent in the world exactly that. Like beauty, taste is determined by the palate of the taster, and one man's *Recheado* is another's *Vindaloo*. Recipes are like dialects of a language; they change with locations. In India, and in particular Goa, both dialects and recipes change every three kilometers as the crow flies.

If you meet an old Goan "Uncle" or "Aunty" (that's the Indian way of respectfully addressing anyone older than yourself), just a few sentences in the local language - Konkani- is enough for them to determine which part of Goa you're from. If you're lucky enough to meet a truly experienced person, they can narrow it down to a village, and with a few prodding questions like, "What's your surname?" and "Do you know so and so?" they might, nay, they will—trace your entire lineage and maybe even introduce you to family members you weren't aware of.

Growing up, my cousins and I were used to getting questioned when we were out cycling around the village or climbing trees or out for our evening *passoi* (walk). The most common way of asking who you were was, "*Tum konallo?*" which translates to "who do you belong to?"(The equivalent of the Canadian Maritimes' "Who's yer fader?") and we had to answer with our relationship to our family's patriarch (or matriarch in our case), which would be, "*Mary ge Naatu*," (Mary's grandson). At this point, you would either be left alone or they'd prod further for more information.

To a Westerner, or even an Indian city dweller, these questions might seem personal or even invasive, but in Goa, this is how we formed relationships. It's a typical small town spread over roughly 1,000 square kilometres, where everyone knows everyone, or at least tries to.

The much-loved and extremely famous beach paradise that is Goa is a popular tourist destination. In the past, it formed a part of the "hippie trail", which started in Great Britain, passed through France, Amsterdam, Iran, Afghanistan and Pakistan, to culminate in India. I believe it was the last stop on the trail, though some of the more adventurous and less psychotropically influenced probably ventured further south to Kerala, or maybe Pondicherry (now *Puducherry*). Eventually, they came back and rested in Goa.

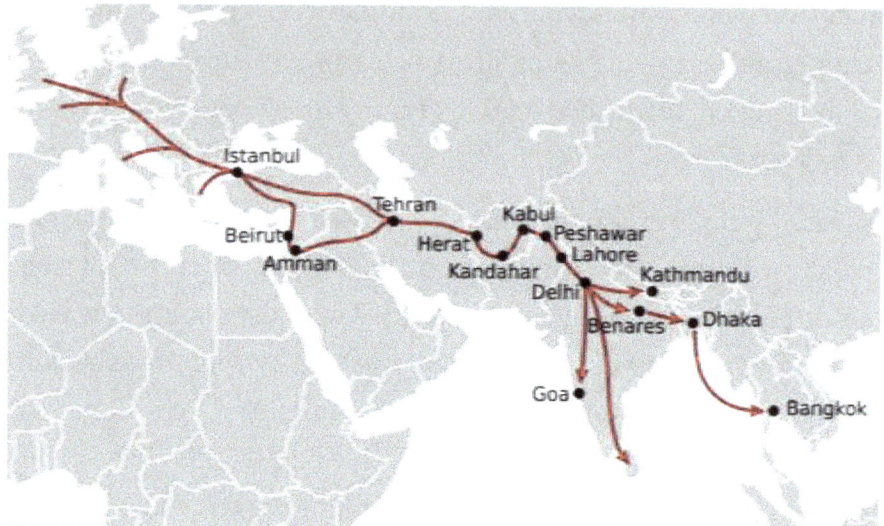

Hippie Trail

The laid-back, mild-tempered locals, who were, after years of Portuguese dominion, used to, and more importantly, indifferent to the antics of the *pakle* (Konkani equivalent of the Mexican Spanish 'gringo'), provided the hippies with a freedom that was hard to find at the time. Wanna go skinny dipping? Sure. How about smoking some weed? No problem. What about a moonlight rave? Go ahead. As long as you don't disturb our way of life or dirty the place, we're good with it, an attitude that is prevalent among Goans even now.

But circling back to the topic of authenticity, how would you classify something as authentic? Especially when everyone's experience is different, even if they live just 100 meters apart? Everyone changes recipes, and even names, to suit their individual preferences. This book documents my personal experiences and my family recipes to give you an insight into my version of "authentic Goa".

Chapter 2:
Sussegado - The Goan Way

I'm not sure of the exact etymology of the word *sussegado* (Portuguese, most likely), but it's now firmly and unmistakably Goan. It refers to a kind of laid-back, laissez-faire, "live and let live" attitude: if it doesn't affect me, I don't care about it. It has its fair share of positives and negatives, about which I could talk for ages, but let's just suffice it to say, it's the way we are in Goa — and, for the most part, we wear it as a badge of honour.

To me, *sussegado* is an afternoon siesta when the sun is too hot to work under. It's sitting in the *balcao* (balcony) in the early evenings, a cup of tea in hand and a sharable plate of *bhojis* (onions in a chickpea batter, deep fried) and *mirchis* (chillies in a chickpea batter, deep fried) by your side while a cool sea breeze gently sways the coconut palms.

It's the five o'clock meeting of men at the local tavern, shooting *feni* (a local liquor made either from coconut sap or the cashew fruit) and sharing more food and even more passionate discourse about football, politics and village affairs (a.k.a. well-seasoned gossip). And finally, it's contentedly sitting down at three in the afternoon to an opulent spread of food which we call Sunday lunch.

Other Indians (non-Goans) interpret *sussegado* as laziness, but it's not at all about being lazy; it's about slowing down and enjoying balance. Goans were never lazy. Historically, most Goans were agriculturists, farmers, fishermen or the like.

In villages, life started early. Everyone was up by 5:00 a.m. (earlier still if you were a baker). The day started with work. A quick chug of *pallea chao* (sweet black tea) and you were either out tending to the fields, pulling in the fishing nets on the beach, climbing coconut trees to tap them for sap (called *toddy*), or milking the cows and goats. Generally, one worked all morning until about 10 o'clock. This was when *pez* (also called *kanji*, much like the Chinese 'congee', is a rice porridge) would be served with pickle or *parra* (a pickled dried fish which is fried before serving). This was meant to fuel workers with carbohydrates for the sweatiest, most gruelling part of the day.

The Goan climate, while undeniably pleasant for holidaymakers, is far from ideal for physical labour. By 11 o'clock, the sun would almost be overhead, and the hours that followed would see the mercury rising fast and furious. Depending on the time of year, it could be anywhere between 28-38 degrees Celsius and with the coastal humidity reaching over eighty percent, one discovers the true meaning of the word sweltering.

The mid-morning work session would last until about 1 or 1:30 in the afternoon when the boost of energy from the *pez* ran out. At this point, the workers would stop for their lunch break — their second fuelling point.

Lunch consisted of the staple fish curry and rice with a few sides like fried fish, some vegetables, pickle and maybe some beans. If you dissect the meal, you'll find the perfect balance of cooking techniques and dietary requirements. There's something poached (fish curry), something steamed/boiled (rice), something sauteed (vegetables) and something fried (again fish, or plantain/potato fritters). From a nutritional standpoint, you have carbohydrates/starch (rice), protein (fish/beans), fats (coconut from the curry and oil from the fried fish), and dietary fibre (vegetables). This was usually accompanied by *solkadi*, a sweet-sourish drink made from the sun-dried skins of the *kokum* (Indian mangosteen) fruit. This drink was infused with additional medicinal herbs and spices, which aid digestion.

The entire peasant meal never really had a formal name. It was called *jevan* in Konkani, which roughly translates to "food" or "meal". In the present day, however, most restaurants have begun calling this a Goan *thali* (the Hindi word for plate).

Goan Fish Thali with Steamed Rice in the centre

Locally, the meal is known as *xit-kodi,* which literally translates to "rice-curry," and it is a general term encompassing both vegetarian and non-vegetarian meals.

While most Goans are non-vegetarian, or at the very least pescatarian, based on their faith/beliefs, there are days and months during which certain foods are off-limits. For most, it's just an abstinence from meat and fish, but for others, it can extend to anything that grows underground (like garlic, onions, etc.). Vegetarians, full-time or just abstaining on a particular day (Hindus generally observe abstinence on certain days of the week or sometimes entire months), would replace the fish curry with a *sourak* (probably a bastardized term for vegetarian - *shivrak*) or a *dal* (lentil stew), and the fried fish would be replaced with fried breadfruit, semolina crusted potatoes or something similar.

Lunch was followed by a siesta. I don't know if this was Portuguese influenced, or whether it was the Goans who influenced them— either way, the siesta provided a respite from the scorching afternoon heat. The siesta usually lasted about an hour, from 2 to 3 p.m., after which the cool sea breeze made it more bearable to continue physical work. The workday usually ended at about 5 p.m., after which the men downed their evening tea before heading to the tavern.

Balcao of a House

The evening tea was — and still is — a time for unwinding. Traditionally, in Goa — or maybe it was just in my family — tea was always consumed sweet and without milk. The milk from our cows and goats was intended for sale, so, except for the children under the age of 10, we didn't drink any ourselves. The evening tea was accompanied by fried snacks, which were usually a type of *bhoji* or the better-known samosa. A *bhoji* is a fritter – a vegetable dipped in a batter of chickpea flour and deep-fried until golden brown. It can be made with anything, although in Goa the main ones you'll find are *mirchi bhoji* (made with chilli peppers), *kandha bhoji* (made with onions) and *kaapa* (made with potatoes). They're eaten either plain or with a coriander chutney (like a 'chimichurri', with coriander/cilantro instead of parsley). Traditionally, these are prepared either at home or at a *gaado* (a roadside kiosk) from which the snacks would be procured fresh and taken home.

Evening tea was family time, or at least it was in my family.

The whole family would gather in the *balcao* and enjoy a few moments of conversation about the day they'd had. The children would run around playing while the adults would chat about politics, or local affairs, peppered with a healthy sprinkling of the latest village scandal, be it an elopement, a land dispute or maybe even an extramarital affair.

After tea, the men would head out to the local tavern while the women prepared dinner and the children played outdoors until dusk.

While the men were finishing at the tavern, the women and children were home having their own "healthy" food. You see, 6 p.m. in Goa was soup time. The mothers and grandmothers would bring out a simple soup consisting of chicken or beef stock, pasta (usually macaroni), and a type of spinach called *vouchi bhaji*. In my house, we used alphabet pasta in the soup. And when chicken stock and alphabet macaroni were hard to come by, we'd have *pez* instead.

Chapter 3:
The Goan Homestead

My Goan homestead evolved during my childhood, as my father and uncles became more financially secure. My family's story is a complex one. Something we don't talk about much for reasons I don't fully understand — whether it be trauma, shame, apathy, or a mix of the above. Luckily, I know enough to explain our homestead and way of life.

A Goan House

Not all Goan houses are built the same, and in order to understand ours, one needs to appreciate the culture surrounding the Goan family. Goans believed in a joint family, which meant that you'd have generations and generations of family living together for as long as the family home could sustain it.

The society is patriarchal. So, the males stay in the family home, while the women are married into other families, which they adopt as their own. While they remain in touch with their birth families, for all traditional and ritualistic purposes, they are no longer a part of it.

Before I go any further, I must emphasize that Goa – and India as a whole – is a land of extremes. On one hand, many old practices are still prevalent, while on the other, an equal number of families and individuals have moved to a modern and inclusive lifestyle. I can only speak from my own experience, writing this from my house in New Brunswick, Canada. I'm a lapsed Catholic who has given up their rights to any ancestral claims and has abandoned most traditions and rituals, save those related to food.

For the remainder of this chapter, I am going to focus on my paternal ancestry and the related house with which I am most familiar.

My grandmother, Maria Elena Damelita D'Almeida of the D'Almeida family of Velim, was married to Robert "Ted" Pinto of Assolna. She abandoned her maiden surname and any claim she had over her ancestral property in Velim and became Maria Elena Damelita Pinto. My grandfather, Ted, as everyone (including his own children and nephews) called him, was the older of two brothers. The house in which they lived was (as per the stories I'm told) the first house of the Pintos clan. The house was built in 1920 on land that was owned by the *Prabhus*, which was our clan's original surname before we were converted to Christianity by the inquisitioning Portuguese (more about that in the following chapters). My grandfather, his brother and their parents all lived together in this house. The house itself was built in the old Portuguese (or more accurately Colonial Goan) style. It had no foundation — it was built on a kind of slab or plinth which rose 6 feet above the ground. The walls were built with *chireem* (large laterite stones cut into 1-foot-high, 18-inch-wide cuboids), and were about 12 feet high. These were then capped by a roof frame built with a mix of teak and coconut tree wood rafters, which were treated with the sap of the cashew tree in order to protect them from termites and water damage. Even though the walls were about 12 feet high, the house was single-storey. The height helped keep the houses cool in summer by allowing for the warmer air to rise. Roofing tiles were imported from Mangalore, in Karnataka, transported by sea and up the river Sal, the banks of which seat the village of Assolna. The river and its associated trade route went all the way up to the city of Margao, the commercial hub of Goa.

The walls were plastered with *chunam* (quicklime), which was produced in the neighbouring village of Chinchinim. They had the *chunnam bhatti*, a kiln where the shells of clams, oysters, and mussels were burnt down to manufacture the white quicklime.

When viewed from the top, the house resembled a large rectangle, housing within it a second, smaller rectangle in the middle. The middle rectangle was an open space called the *rosangan* (literal translation: rosegarden) . This was a kitchen garden where vegetables and herbs were grown. The back of the house had the kitchen to one side and the toilet on the other. The toilet opened into the pig sty (I believe the technical term is "toilets serviced by animals") while the kitchen opened into the backyard, where the other animals were kept when they weren't out on their grazing walks.

When you faced the front of the house, you were greeted by a flight of stairs that took you into a covered porch we called a *balcao*. Hexagonal in shape, the *balcao* had enough seating for at least 16. The far end of the *balcao* led to a verandah on either side, which wrapped the entire front and sides of the house. The roof of the house extended over the *balcao*. The verandahs had multiple four-paneled (in two rows of two) doors for access. These doors were and are a hallmark of Goan-Portuguese architecture. Set into arched openings in the stone walls, the doors were made of a combination of wood and mother-of-pearl. While the wood formed the framework, the mother-of-pearl was the perfect material to filter out the harsh sunlight. The design of the doors was such that they could be used as windows by opening only the top two panels, or as doors when you opened the bottom two as well. These kinds of doors and windows still adorn a few Goan houses and are considered works of art.

At the far end of the *balcao* stood the front doors to the house, which opened into the *entrada* (entrance). This room housed the altar with all its religious iconography. The altar was made of teak wood and was covered with an "altar cloth", embroidered with a bible verse and images of doves or flowers of some sort.

14

This shrine housed a crucifix, a statue of Mary, at least one picture of the Sacred Heart of Jesus and Mary, statues of the patron saints of the family, and an oil lamp and candles (that were later replaced with electric lights that imitated the flickering of a flame).

On either side of the *entrada* were the *salas* (halls). These were for entertainment and parties, and they opened onto the verandahs through the four-panelled doors described earlier.

Past the *entrada* was the *rosangan* surrounded by a corridor on all sides. The corridor only had walls on its outer edges; the inner side was open and contained stairs, at intervals, that descended to the *rosangan* at ground level. The bedrooms lined the outer sides of the left and right corridors, and at the far end of the *rosangan*, the corridor opened into the pantry and kitchen.

This was the original layout of the house. After my grandfather and his father passed, my granduncle's wife couldn't get along with my grandmother, and the house was partitioned – a wall was built through the middle of the house, dividing the *entrada* and the kitchen. The *balcao, rosangan* and the backyard were shared. But for privacy, a wall with multiple windows was built around the *rosangan,* closing up the open side of the corridor. Years later, subsequent renovations were made on our side of the house to modernize it.

The house was designed for functionality based on what was available and affordable at the time. Take, for example, bathing or washing up. Bathing is something that Goans do a little differently from the rest of India. The rest of India tends to bathe in the mornings, while Goans (at least everyone that I knew) bathed at night. The thought was to get rid of the day's sweat and grime and be fresh and cool for a good night's sleep.

The bath itself was something of an experience. Now, throughout my lifetime, I've been lucky enough to see economic prosperity, which has afforded us upgrades in our bathrooms. In the very beginning, we bathed by the well. We'd draw water from the well with a *colso* (a brass pot with a lipped neck around which a hangman's noose was tied so as to lower it into the well to draw water), and pour the nice cool water over ourselves. This was for the young boys who could bare their bodies without their "dignity" being impeded in any way. For the girls and women, it was a bit more tedious. They had a kind of private cubicle, a few meters away between the kitchen and the banana grove (every house had one), where they would bathe. They had to draw water from the same well, pour it into a bucket that they'd carry to the cubicle bathroom. As such, they needed to draw the exact amount of water they would need or ration the water they drew.

The cubicle was also used by the males when it was too cold to have a "cold water bath." The wall of the cubicle that faced the kitchen was only waist-high. Just outside this wall, in the kitchen, sat a large cauldron, positioned so it could be reached from the bathing cubicle. This cauldron would be filled with water that was kept heated by a fire beneath it throughout the evening. We used this hot water to temper the well water in the bucket for a pleasant, warm bath.

On a side note, when I say bath, I don't imply the use of a tub. We did not have those. We'd scoop water from the bucket using a small brass tumbler (or later in life, a plastic mug), pour the water over our bodies, lather our bodies with soap, and rinse once again using the tumbler.

As our family's financial situation improved, we were able to afford indoor plumbing and the bathing cubicle was converted into a complete indoor bathroom. An overhead tank was installed with an electric pump that connected it to the well. The overhead tank would be filled once a day, and that would provide gravity-fed water to the faucets in the kitchen and bathroom. Grey water from the kitchen and bathroom was directed to the banana grove, as those plants need a lot of water.

Later in life, as the family prospered economically, we built more bathrooms and even toilets as we could now afford a septic tank and a soak pit. The soak pit was built in the banana grove itself, and the septic tank was built at the edge of the property across from the well. I remember the positioning of the two being a huge bone of contention in the family. At the time, there were no real experts, and everyone had an opinion. The internet being non-existent, we had to rely on the knowledge of the most qualified person in the village, which happened to be the registrar, and even he wasn't sure. So, then the doctor was consulted (engineers were unheard of in the village at the time). Finally, my dad, being a captain on a ship, consulted with one of his chief engineers and got the thing built. We now had showers with running hot water! This was around the early 80's.

PART 2:

THE

GOAN

KITCHEN

Chapter 4:
The Evolution of
the Kitchen

Ten years ago, it would have been hard to believe that households would exist without fully equipped kitchens, but in the present day, it's a reality. The breakaway from the hetero-normative family, coupled with more intense workloads and easy availability of take-out and delivery options, renders the kitchen rather redundant. Most families only need a microwave, fridge, dishwasher, and maybe a couple of other pieces of equipment. Historically, however, more time was spent in the kitchen than in any other room in a house, and this is especially true in Goa. Most Goan kitchens were add-ons to the back of the house. They had large gaps below the roof to allow for ventilation. There was no running water, and heat was generated through a wood fire fuelled by coconut husks, dry leaves, and any other dry vegetation found around the garden or property.

The Traditional Goan Kitchen

Our kitchen had three hearths — one for the large cauldron of water, which was shared with the bathroom cubicle, and the other two were on a raised counter for cooking. Above the counter-top hearths was a long bamboo pole suspended horizontally from the roof. From this bamboo pole hung braided onions and garlic, sausages, dried fish, and other dry herbs and spices. Since this was above the wood fire, everything that was hung from the pole was constantly being smoked, which preserved them longer.

To the right of the hearth was the doorway and stairs that led to the backyard. My grandmother, mother or I would sit at the *adolli* at the top of the stairs. The *adolli* is one of those old-school, simple instruments that are still used in a lot of Goan households. It consists of a low rectangular bench about eighteen inches high. One of the shorter ends of the bench tapers into a triangle (or semi-circle), the point of which has a curved steel blade on a hinge attached to it. This sickle-shaped (but much wider) blade is used to clean fish, pry open mussel and clam shells, cut food and more. The blade ends in a flat multi-pointed star perpendicular to the blade. This is the grating head, used to grate coconut. The hinge allows you to fold the blade over the bench so that the grating head rests flat on the bench and the dull side of the blade faces upwards — a simple design that reduces the risk of injury when it is not in use. The *adolli* was the primary instrument used for cleaning fish, grating coconut, and any kind of cutting.

The Adolli with an open blade

To the left of the stairs, adjacent to the back door, was the grinding stone. Goa has two kinds of grinding stones, the *rogdo* and the *phator*. Both of these are made from granite and are used to grind spice pastes. The *rogdo* is a much larger 'molcajete' (Mexican mortar and pestle with the pestle being only slightly smaller than the hole in the mortar. The *phator* (our choice of grinding stone) is like the Aztec 'metate', and consists of a flat piece of granite with grooves chipped into it, and a cylindrical roller that you had to drag to and fro over the spices, to create a paste.

Using the *fator* was my first experience with cooking. I must've been five years old at the time, and being mischievous, I got into some kind of trouble. As punishment, my grandmother decided that I would grind the chilli and spice paste for that afternoon's meal. Grinding involved handling the paste with your bare hand (gloves were unheard of), and since the main ingredients in the paste are chilli, garlic, ginger and pepper, any micro cuts or nicks on your hand would burn on contact. It was a punishment that left the sting lingering for hours, even after you'd washed your hands.

The Rogdo

The Fator

Beside the kitchen was what we called the "store room", but was technically a pantry. This is where the bulk of the food was stored: grains, nuts, coconut oil, vinegar, sweets, pickles, beans, rice, flour, and also some cooking equipment. Most of the food was stored in large ceramic jars that were glazed halfway in a yellowish-brown colour, while leaving the rest greyish-white. These are iconic storage containers and were used for anything that needed to be kept dry, away from humidity. Grains were stored in either *shempuls* (cane baskets) or large cylindrical aluminium tins (repurposed oil tins) with press-fit lids.

Today, the traditional Goan kitchen exists only in museums and in the memories of those who lived through it. The wood fires have been replaced by natural gas stoves and ranges, and the horizontal bamboo pole is no longer used, thanks to refrigerators and year-round availability of supplies. The large water cauldron has been replaced by modern water heaters (electric, solar) and indoor plumbing. Not wholly or in full measure, but very substantially, the *adolli* and grinding stones have been replaced by knives and electric food processors. There still exist a few who have held on to the old tools and do things the traditional way, quoting phrases like "old is gold" or insisting that the kind of flavour you get from the *rogdo* doesn't compare to the food processor. I happen to be one of those, but whether there really is a difference in flavour or if it is the physical manifestation of the romanticized memories of the past, I cannot say.

Chapter 5:
The Goan Pantry

If you're cooking Goan food, there are a few ingredients you'll want to keep on hand. Goan cuisine is vibrant, rich, and aromatic, drawing influences from India, Portugal, and local coastal traditions. Some ingredients you'll need in whole spice form for toasting and grinding, while others you'll want as convenient powders or ready-to-use pastes.

Over the years, I've honed some of these recipes so they can be made even if you don't own a spice grinder. However, some of them can't be modified, so having a spice grinder or a food processor is definitely recommended to unlock the freshest flavours. A good grinder, you can grind spices (after toasting) just before cooking, releasing aromas that transform a dish from good to unforgettable.

The average Goan pantry typically includes the following (the Goan terms are provided in brackets):

Spices

Pepper *(Miri)*:

By far the most common—and underrated—spice in Goan cuisine. No matter what savoury dish you make, it's almost certain to include pepper. When used whole, it imparts flavour without much heat, but when powdered, it delivers both heat and flavour. Pepper heat is different from chilli heat: chilli heat hits the back of your throat and tongue, while pepper creates a slight tingling on your lips and in the corners of your mouth. Depending on the recipe, you could need it whole or as a powder.

Cumin *(Jeerem)*:

One of the most important spices in Goan cooking, it lends an earthy, slightly herbaceous taste to dishes. When tempered in hot oil, it releases a distinct fragrance that adds depth to the flavour. Depending on the recipe, you might need whole cumin seeds or ground cumin — but in a pinch, ground cumin alone will suffice.

Turmeric *(Haldi/Halad)*:

This spice is used more for its vibrant colour and health benefits than for flavour. Traditionally, turmeric was an antiseptic — if you had a wound, you'd apply turmeric to help it heal. For skin conditioning, a turmeric-sandalwood paste was commonly used. Turmeric and salt were used for preserving meat. Turmeric has a bitter, pungent taste when used in large quantities; however, the recipes in this book require only ground turmeric in modest amounts.

Kashmiri Red Chilli *(Kashmiri Sanga)*:

These chillies are among the mildest available. However, they lend a brilliant red color to any dish they're used in. Most recipes in this book use the powdered form. If you can't find

Kashmiri chilli powder, substitute a 1:1 blend of paprika and cayenne pepper, or adjust the ratio to your taste.

On a side note, chillies are what we in India refer to what North America calls hot peppers.

Baidgi Chillies (*Shempda Sanga*):

These chillies are used for heat. They can be hard to find, so cayenne pepper is a good substitute. The recipes in this book use them in powdered form.

Cloves (*Karafulam*):

These little scepter-like buds bring a distinctive fragrance and a sweet warmth to dishes. They're essential for many Goan recipes, contributing both balance and complexity.

Cardamom (*Elchi/Velchi*):

Cardamom imparts a hint of sweetness and an almost menthol-like cooling sensation. Its floral aroma, with a slight heat, makes it popular in sweets for a complex sweetness, though it's also used in some savoury dishes.

Coriander Seeds (*Sambhar*):

Coriander adds earthiness, freshness and subtle herbaceous notes. You typically need more coriander seeds than other spices, as they balance the stronger flavours (example: the earthiness of cumin). Most of my recipes call for ground coriander seeds.

Cinnamon *(Tiki)*:

The reason for Europe's interest in India and the reason America was discovered. This beautiful spice adds a sweet-spiciness that confuses, yet delights. A little goes a long way with cinnamon, and some of my recipes call for the sticks, while others use ground cinnamon.

Nutmeg *(Zaiphal)*:

Wonderfully aromatic, nutmeg provides a sweet, earthy note. It is used sparingly as large quantities can cause hallucinations and even be fatal. As Anthony Bourdain once said, "the best food is the one that offers at least some risk." [wink]

Mace *(Patri)*:

Mace comes from the same plant as nutmeg and is the lacy membrane that surrounds the nutmeg seed. It has a similar but milder flavour than nutmeg, and is used whole in my recipes.

Star Anise *(Dongraful)*:

This is a rather beautiful spice. It looks like a woody flower with six to eight petals. It has a strong aniseed flavour, but is milder than licorice. You need these whole.

Fenugreek Seeds *(Methi)*:

Bitter with a herbaceous aftertaste, fenugreek adds balance to many dishes. You'll need these as whole seeds.

Mustard Seeds *(Saasam/Rye)*:

The mildly peppery taste that these impart, along with the nutty flavour when tempered, gives a unique flavour to food. You will need these whole, and preferably the red/black ones rather than the white ones.

Curry Leaves *(Karipatta)*:

A beautiful spice that offers a peppery herbaceous flavour that is unmatched by any other spice. Often used to flavour oil or ground into pastes, curry leaves are best used fresh, though dried leaves can be used instead.

Indian Bay Leaves *(Tiki Panam)*:

Unlike the bay leaves used in Western cuisine, these come from the cinnamon tree and are spicier and sweeter than Bay Laurel leaves. Indian bay leaves are usually used whole, just like their Western counterparts.

Base Ingredients

Now, let's take a closer look at the basic ingredients—the humble building blocks that bring each dish to life with flavour, warmth, and tradition.

Every cuisine has its aromatic base—whether it's 'mirepoix', 'sofrito', or the Holy Trinity. In Goan cuisine, the base is typically ginger, garlic, and onion. In Konkani, we call this *fond*, a term likely borrowed from Portuguese, meaning "foundation."

Ginger *(Allem)*:

Earthy, spicy and fragrant, depending on the dish you're making, you could need this whole or ground.

Garlic *(Lasoon)*:

The best-tasting ingredient that's universally recognized and used. And even though the late Queen of England had a disdain for it, it's the base of all Indian, nay, Asian cuisine. The cardinal rule: one clove of garlic per person served. My recipes require it whole, in paste or powder form.

Onions/Shallots *(Peeyao)*:

Essential for thickening, flavouring, and forming the base of nearly every Goan dish. Shallots are preferred for authentic Goan cuisine, but red onions work well too. Yellow or white onions won't produce quite the same flavour, but can be used as alternates as well.

Tomatoes *(Tomat)*:

This is used far less than the others and may even be skipped. I like using fresh Roma tomatoes, and find they work best.

Thickeners

In most Goan cooking, thickeners aren't required. Spice pastes and the *fond* usually thicken gravies sufficiently. However, in some cases, these thickeners are used:

Coconut (*Naal*, the grated version is called *Chun* or *Soi*, and the young coconut is called *Adsol*):

Coconut is predominantly used in its freshly grated form. Avoid desiccated coconut, which lacks the moisture and has a very different flavour from fresh coconut. Grated fresh coconut can usually be found in the freezer section of Asian grocery stores.

Coconut Cream (*Roce*):

Obtained by grinding coconut and collecting the extracted liquid, coconut cream is used primarily for flavour, but also acts as a thickener. I highly recommend canned coconut creams from Thailand for convenience and quality.

Other Ingredients

Coconut Vinegar (*Vinagre*):

Made from the sap of the coconut tree, coconut vinegar is the preferred souring agent in Goan cuisine and offers similar health benefits to apple cider vinegar. It's commonly found in Filipino grocery stores. If unavailable, apple cider vinegar is a decent substitute.

Tamarind (*Aamsand*):

Another souring agent, it can be used in its pulp form, paste form or dried form.

Kokum *(Binda Solam)*:

The dried skin of Indian Mangosteen, it is another souring agent used in Goan cooking.

Bilimbis *(Bimbli)*:

A rare ingredient in Europe and America, though you may find it in dried (needing re-hydration before use) or frozen form at Bangladeshi stores.

Note:

The souring agent used depends on the dish. Generally, kokum or bilimbis are best when cooking for same-day consumption, as they provide immediate sourness without intensifying upon reheating. For food intended for the next day, tamarind or vinegar is preferred, as their acidity intensifies over time and helps preserve the food.

Coconut Jaggery *(Ghod)*:

Coconut Jaggery is unprocessed coconut sugar, and it adds sweetness along with an earthy, nutty flavour. It is traditionally available in lump form with a sticky, almost play-dough-like texture. In North America, it's often sold in powdered form as coconut sugar.

Bread *(Pao)*:

Though not an integral part of the Goan Pantry, bread is widely used in Goa. Not to be confused with popular Indian flatbreads like 'naan' or 'roti', Goan bread is leavened and is similar to what would be called a roll in North America.

Chapter 6:
Everyday Staples

Every cuisine has its staples. For the Italians, it's probably pasta, for most Asians, it's rice and curry, and for others, it may be a stew or a soup. The Goan staple is fish curry and rice. But along with that, we do have a few other dishes which could be considered staples.

Pao

Pao in Konkani refers to bread, but is also a slur used by Mumbaikars (people who live in Mumbai) to refer to Goans. We've now adopted it with pride, after all, without *paos*, half of Mumbai's street food would be non-existent. From the now world famous *vada pao*: a chickpea batter coated spiced potato patty, deep fried and served in the hollowed out center of a *pao* (bread) with some powdered garlic chutney, or maybe a liquid coconut chutney; to *pao bhaji*: a typically Mumbai vegetable mash curry served with fresh onions, a squeeze of lime and a dollop of butter, and of course a side of toasted *pao*; none of these would exist if Goan bakers from the small village of Saligao hadn't travelled to Mumbai and started baking for the city.

Assortment of Goan Bread

Pao is a general term as well as a specific one. When used in general, it refers to any type of bread (including sliced, which most Goans will use only for sandwiches). When used specifically, it refers to a type of bread, one made with refined flour. The *pao* has a leathery outer crust but is soft and airy on the inside. It looks like a roll but is the size of a bun. The bread is usually made in a batch of 6 loaves, which join together to form pull-away bread, and is sold individually. You get two varieties, *moh pao* and *kadak pao,* which translates to soft bread and crisp bread, respectively. The other popular varieties of bread include:

Katre pao: A butterfly-shaped, fully crusted loaf of bread about the size of one's fist. It gets its name from the tool that is used to make the shape. After the dough has risen the first time, it is punched out and made into small balls. For *Katre pao*, the balls are cut using scissors *(kator* in Konkani) halfway through the sphere, and then the ball is turned inside out at the cut and the corners spread out to form a butterfly or bow-tie shape. This kind of bread is usually hollow inside like a pita, and works very well for stuffing with gravy dishes as a snack to go.

Undo (plural: *unde; pouse* in South Goa): A dense bread with a hard crust. It is usually hemispherical in shape with a slit across the crust. *Unde* is higher in fibre than *pao*, as it is usually made with a mixture of whole wheat flour and refined flour and sometimes even a little wheat bran.

Poiee/bhakri: The Goan brown bread. Made from mainly whole wheat flour and wheat bran, it is a flatbread, round in shape. Before baking, it is coated with even more wheat bran, giving it a rough, fibrous exterior. *Poiee*, like *katre pao*, is hollow inside and is great for making pocket sandwiches. If you're in the South, *bhakri* and *poiee* are interchangeable terms, but in the North, *bhakri* refers to an unleavened bread more commonly known throughout India as *chapati* or *roti*.

Kankon (translates to "bangle"): As its name suggests, it is a bangle/doughnut-shaped bread. It's actually a soup stick in the form of a ring. It's meant to be dipped and eaten, and is usually had in the mornings with tea or at night with soup. It's not found much anymore as regular soup sticks have taken their place, but as a child, it was a fun way to have soup with an edible bangle around your wrist.

Bol: A coconut bread made with coconut and jaggery. It's different in North Goa and South Goa. In the South, it has a brioche-like consistency and is made with flour and coconut milk with a few chunks of fresh coconut. In the North, it refers to a dense, cake-like sweet made with grated coconut and jaggery with the colour of a brownie.

Lambe pao (translates to "long bread"): A regular *pao*, but shaped like a hot dog bun. Once again, you get these in *kadak* and *moh* variants.

Traditionally, bread-making in Goa didn't use yeast; they used toddy (*sur*) instead. The toddy, being sweet, fermented fast and made the bread rise. Contemporarily, though, toddy is a rare commodity, and between its use in *feni* and coconut vinegar, there isn't enough to go into bread. Moreover, yeast is now cheap and makes the end product more affordable.

The breads of Goa are unique and tasty. It's something most people who try instantly fall in love with, and for good reason. The textures and consistency of *paos* make it uniquely suited to mop up the rich, spicy gravies of Goan cooking, be it the dark, sweet-spicy *sorpotel* gravy or the thick, textured coconut gravy of a *xacuti*, or even the thinner, spicy gravy of the *ambot-tik*. It doesn't matter what you're eating; a *pao* just enhances it.

An important part of Goan culture is the "breadman" (the superhero who delivers your bread) called the *poder*. Literally, the term *poder* translates to "baker", but it's used most often to address the bread delivery person. The *poders* travel from the bakery throughout neighbourhoods in Goa, selling bread house-to-house on bicycles equipped with a large cane basket at the back, which holds the bread. They use a bladder horn to alert residents to their arrival, and when you hear the distinctive "ponk ponk" of the horn, you know it's time to rush out to buy bread.

Goa's Superhero – the Poder – making sure you always have your meal on time

Goan Pao

Specific Equipment:

Stand mixer with dough hook attachment

Ingredients (makes 18 loaves):

- 1 kg All-Purpose Flour
- 600 g Water
- 1 tsp Salt
- 2 tsp Active Dry Yeast

Method:

1. Place the water in the bowl of the stand mixer.

2. Add in the yeast and set aside for about 10 minutes to let the yeast bloom.

3. Add in the flour and salt, and begin kneading using the dough hook attachment.

4. Knead for at least 10 minutes. The dough should form a uniform mass.

5. Cover with a towel and set it in a warm place to rise (about 1 to 1 ½ hours, depending on the temperature).

6. Once the dough doubles in size, punch out the air and divide the dough into 90 g portions.

7. Form each portion into a ball by rolling it in your floured hands.

8. Place them in a baking tin about 2 inches apart.

9. Cover with a plastic sheet and leave in a warm place for about 45 minutes.

10. Place a bowl of water on the bottom rack of the oven.

11. Preheat the oven to 450°F.

12. Place the bread on the top rack and bake for 18-20 minutes until golden brown on top.

Poiee/Bhakri

Specific Equipment:

Stand mixer with dough hook attachment

Ingredients (makes 18 loaves):

- 500 g All-Purpose Flour
- 500 g Whole Wheat Flour
- 2 Tbsp Millet Flour
- 1 cup + 2 Tbsp Wheat Bran
- 650 g Water
- 1 tsp Salt
- 2 tsp Active Dry Yeast

Method:

1. Place the water in the bowl of the stand mixer.
2. Add in the yeast and set aside for about 10 minutes to let the yeast bloom.
3. Add in the flours, salt and 2 Tbsp wheat bran, and begin kneading using the dough hook attachment.
4. Knead for at least 10 minutes. The dough should form a uniform mass.
5. Cover with a towel and set it in a warm place to rise (about 1 to 1 ½ hours, depending on the temperature).

6. Once the dough doubles in size, punch out the air and divide the dough into 90 g portions.

7. Preheat the oven to 400°F.

8. Pour the remaining wheat bran onto a flat plate.

9. Form each portion of dough into a ball.

10. Place a dough ball on the wheat bran and press down to flatten. Coat the other side as well.

11. Roll the dough into a 4-inch disc using a rolling pin.

12. Repeat steps 10 and 11 for the remaining dough balls.

13. Place the discs on a baking tray.

14. Place the baking tray in the oven for 15 minutes (or until the flatbreads puff up like balloons).

Masala

The word "masala" can be confusing to anyone not born or brought up in India. Masala probably derives from the Sanskrit word 'mas', meaning spices. It could also have been borrowed from Persian, where the word means ingredients. Today, the word is used in India in many different contexts, each with its own meaning. The challenge of translating languages is that it is often impossible to have a word-for-word translation, and this is one such case. You see, masala can be used to indicate a spice blend ('chaat masala' or 'garam masala'). It is used in dish names ('channa masala'). It can indicate a spice paste (*recheado masala*). Or it can be used to represent spiciness ('masala chai'). Outside food, it is also used to denote something upbeat or lively (Bollywood masala) or even gossip (what's the latest masala). So defining it is difficult, if not impossible. It's, as they say, a vibe.

Culinarily, though, I would define a masala as a spice blend, either wet or dry, which cannot be consumed by itself or as a condiment. It's something that needs to be processed or added to a dish to complete it. There are exceptions, of course, which you will see during the course of this book.

Masala is the Indian equivalent of the French mother sauces. It's what forms the base of our entire cuisine. Goan cuisine also includes several condiments that can be classified as one of two types: chutneys and pickles.

Chutneys are very similar to masalas as they are also a combination of different spices ground together. They can be in the form of powders or pastes. The difference between chutneys and masalas is that chutneys are usually consumed as condiments and are "ready to eat", while masalas form a part of a dish.

Pickles are basically preserved meats, fruits or vegetables. Most of the Western world associates the word pickles with cucumbers in brine. In India, however, pickles refer to the preservation of the primary ingredient through acidification in an aromatic paste that is often spicy. In Goa, the vegetarian pickles are collectively called *lonchem,* with each of them having individual names.

Now I get to an important point of discussion: the word "curry".

Curry is a term that is used a lot in Indian cuisine. Let's unpack this word a bit. Curry is NOT a single dish, and curry powder is NOT an Indian invention. Curry in India just refers to a gravy or sauce, and each dish has its individual name, like butter chicken, vindaloo, etc. They're all curries. And if it's a new recipe you're inventing, you can give it your own name. Like in my family, my grandmother's chicken curry was very well-liked and was called Nana Mary's chicken curry. With influences from the rest of the world and our well-documented anglophilia, the word has made its way back to India and Goa, leading to a proliferation of dishes with "curry" in the name – like the Goan fish curry or the Kerala 'meen curry'. These curries had their own names at some point, but with time, they've been replaced.

In the rest of this chapter, I share recipes for the daily staples of Goan Cuisine.

Rice

Rice is the most important dish in Goan cuisine. You may have the best of meats and fish on the table, but if there's no rice, there's no meal. Rice is probably the simplest thing to cook, but for anyone who is not familiar with it, it can seem daunting.

Rice – Cook and Drain Method

Specific Equipment:

Colander

Ingredients (serves 2):

- 1 cup Rice
- 4 cups of Water, plus more for washing
- 3 tsp Salt

Method:

1. Wash the rice a couple of times to get rid of the husk and other dirt.

2. Place the rice in a pot and cover with 4 cups of cold water.

3. Add in the salt and place the pot on the stove at medium heat, uncovered.

4. Once the water begins boiling, wait for 10 minutes and then check the rice by taking a few grains and squeezing them between your fingers. They should offer some resistance, but smash to a paste easily. This means they're done. If they are not, continue boiling and check after another 5 minutes.

5. Take the pot off the stove and drain it using a colander.

Pro tip:

The starchy water, which is drained from the rice, can be drunk as an energy drink. In the old days, we used this water to starch our clothes for that crisp look.

Generally, the rice takes about 15 minutes to cook after the water comes to a boil. However, this will depend on the variety of rice you are using. Basmati, *Colum*, Calrose and Jasmine rice cook faster (within about 5-10 minutes of boiling), whereas wild rice, brown rice, and black rice take longer (up to 20 minutes of boiling).

Rice - Cover and Absorb Method

This is another method to cook rice and does not require a colander. It takes roughly the same amount of time on the stove, but it uses less water.

Specific Equipment:

Pot with lid

Ingredients (serves 2):

- 1 cup Rice
- 2 cups of Water, plus more for washing
- 1 tsp Salt

Method:

1. Wash the rice thoroughly. In this method, we have to ensure that all the loose starch from the rice is washed away. You can wash the rice in a colander under running water until the water that drains is no longer milky, or you can wash it in a pot by submerging the rice under water, agitating by hand and draining. Usually, you will need to repeat the process about 5 to 7 times or until the water stops turning milky when you agitate the rice.

2. Place the washed rice in the pot, add the water and salt, cover with the lid and place it on low/medium heat.

3. Let it cook for about 15 minutes, and then check to see if the water is absorbed by the rice – this can be determined by keeping an eye out for holes forming on the top of the rice (the holes form to allow the steam to release). Turn off the heat and keep the pot covered for another 10 minutes. This allows the rice to absorb the remaining water without overcooking it.

Curry

Curries in Goa are usually coconut-based (much like Thai curries). The use of *soi/chun* (grated coconut) and *roce* (coconut milk) is almost mandatory. There are a few curries that do not use coconut in any form, but these are made for lighter meals.

Goan Fish Curry - Whole Ingredients

Specific Equipment:

Mixer-grinder or food processor

Ingredients (serves 4-6):

- 500 g Fish, cut into 50 g pieces (The most common fish used is mackerel, but can be replaced with most strong-flavoured, firm-flesh fish like king fish, barracuda, snapper, mullets, etc. Preferably use saltwater fish and not freshwater fish).

- 400 ml Coconut Cream (or 1 cup grated Coconut)

- Water

- 5 Kashmiri Red Chillies (10 g)

- 2 Thai Green Chillies (optional)

- 6 cloves of Garlic

- 1 inch Ginger, peeled

- 1 tsp Cumin

- 1 tsp Coriander Seeds

- ¼ tsp Turmeric powder

- ½-1 tsp Salt

- 3-4 *Tephal* (Indian peppers) whole (optional)

- 1 tsp Tamarind paste or 2-3 Kokum pieces

- 1 Onion or 2 Shallots

- 1 Tbsp Oil

Method:

1. Wash the fish and season it with salt and turmeric powder. Set aside in the fridge covered for 1 hour or until needed.

2. In a mixer grinder or food processor, grind the Kashmiri chillies, ginger, garlic, cumin, and coriander seeds together with about 2 Tbsp of water. If using grated coconut and tamarind, add these as well. Grind until it forms a smooth paste. This is your curry paste, which can be frozen in an airtight jar for up to 3 months.

3. Slice the onions into thin slices (a Julienne slice, which is ⅛ inch or less in width).

4. In a saucepan or stock pot, add the oil and place over a medium-high heat.

5. Add in the onions and sauté until they just start to caramelize.

6. Now pour in the curry paste and lower the heat to the low setting.

7. If using coconut cream instead of grated coconut, add the coconut cream.

8. Add water to the pot until the mixture has the viscosity you are aiming for.

9. If using kokum instead of tamarind paste, add the kokum.

10. Now add in the Indian peppers and the Thai green chillies (if using).

11. Once the curry starts bubbling, taste it for seasoning. Add salt or tamarind paste/kokum as needed.

12. Drop the pieces of fish into the curry carefully. Once the fish is added, do not stir using a spoon, as that may cause the pieces of fish to break apart. Instead, shake the entire saucepan/pot gently in circular motions to stir.

13. Cover the pot and let it simmer for 10 minutes, shaking the pot occasionally to ensure the fish doesn't stick to the base.

14. Serve over rice.

Notes:

1. These are the general recipes for fish curry that are used in most Goan Catholic households. Of course, everyone has their own spin on it, and you can try adding your own.

2. The same curry paste can be used for different protein/vegetable combinations. Traditionally, this curry was only made with seafood, eggs or some vegetables, the most popular proteins being fish, shrimp/prawns, okra, and eggs (either poached in the gravy or boiled and then added after peeling off the shell). When in season, green (unripe) mango is

sometimes added, and during the monsoons, dried shrimp/prawns used to replace fresh shrimp/prawns (as fresh shrimp/prawns were hard to come by).

Goan Fish Curry - Ground/Powdered Ingredients

Ingredients (serves 4-6):

- 500 g Fish, cut into 50 g pieces (The most common fish used is mackerel, but can be replaced with most strong-flavoured firm-flesh fish like king fish, barracuda, snapper, mullets, etc. Preferably, use saltwater fish and not freshwater fish.)
- 400 ml Coconut Cream
- Water
- 2 Tbsp Kashmiri Chilli powder
- 2 Thai Green Chillies (optional)
- 1 Tbsp granulated Garlic
- 1½ tsp Ginger powder
- 1 tsp Cumin powder
- 1 tsp Coriander powder
- ¼ tsp Turmeric powder
- ½-1 tsp Salt
- 3-4 *Tephal* (Indian peppers) whole (optional)
- 1 tsp Tamarind paste or 2-3 Kokum pieces

- 1 Onion or 2 Shallots
- 1 Tbsp Oil

Method:

1. If using tamarind, soak the tamarind in 2 Tbsp of hot water.

2. Wash the fish, season it with salt and turmeric powder, and set it in the fridge covered for 1 hour or until needed.

3. Pour 2 Tbsp of hot water over the tamarind in a bowl and leave to soak.

4. Slice the onions into thin slices (a Julienne slice, which is ⅛ inch or less in width).

5. In a saucepan or stock pot, add the oil and place over a medium-high heat.

6. Add in the onions and sauté until they just start to caramelize.

7. Mix the Kashmiri chilli powder, ginger, garlic, cumin, and coriander powders together in a bowl.

8. Pour the mixture over the onions and sauté for 5 minutes on low heat.

9. Add in the coconut cream.

10. If using kokum, add it to the pot. If using tamarind, wring out all the juices of the tamarind into the water it was soaking in. Discard the wrung tamarind and pour the tamarind water into the pot.

11. Add water to the pot until the mixture has the viscosity you are aiming for.

12. Now add in the Indian peppers and the Thai green chillies (if using).

13. Once the curry starts bubbling, taste it for seasoning. Add salt or tamarind paste/kokum as needed.

14. Drop the pieces of fish into the curry carefully. Once the fish is added, do not stir using a spoon, as that may cause the pieces of fish to break apart. Instead, shake the entire saucepan/pot gently in circular motions to stir.

15. Cover the pot and let it simmer for 10 minutes, shaking the pot occasionally to ensure the fish doesn't stick to the base.

16. Serve over rice.

The Seafood Sides

Seafood is an important part of Goan Cuisine. We're divided by language, religion, culture, caste and geography, but the one thing that unites us all is a love for seafood. So much so that even during Lent, Catholics will abstain from meat, but fish remains fair game.

Goa lies on the Konkan coast of India and is blessed with abundant fishing grounds. The variety of fish that is eaten ranges from small bait fish (*canarem* or *caduam*), which I believe is a type of minnow, slightly larger ones like *velio* (Indian anchovies), then come the little to mid-sized ones like *tarle* (sardines) or *lepo* (tongue sole) or the infamous *bombil*/bombay duck (lizard fish). On another tangent, there's an interesting reason for the lizard fish being called "Bombay duck", which involves the Indian railway, the stench of dried fish, and the mail. The word for mail in Hindi is 'daak', and the train that travelled from Bombay (now Mumbai) to Calcutta (now Kolkata), which also carried the mail, was called the Bombay Daak (or the Bombay Mail). This train also transported the dried lizard fish from Bombay to Calcutta and gave the train its distinct smell, which the British officers (allegedly) thought smelt like a duck coop. Hence, the train and the fish were named Bombay Duck. Now, back to our fish discussion.

Then there are the mid-sized varieties like *bangdo* (Indian Mackerel), *shyotayo* (mullets) or *mudoshi* (lady fish); and the larger varieties like *visvon* (Indian kingfish or sear fish), *chonak* (giant perch), *tamso* (red snapper), *palu* (rock perch), *rogtado* (tuna), *mori* (shark, usually dog shark or hammerhead), and the biggest one I've ever come across - *gobro* (grouper).

Besides fish, we are also blessed with brackish water oysters (*kalvam*), multiple types of clams (*tisriyo, cundoyom*), mussels, which have different names in the North and South Goa (*shenaniyo* and *zob*, respectively), crabs, lobsters, crayfish, squid, shrimp/prawns and many other types.

The ones named here are probably just 20% of the variety Goans have access to. Each fish or seafood type is prepared differently, and there are rules, unwritten and unspoken, but somehow still set in stone. Any wavering from these is blasphemy, and the resulting dish, however palatable or delicious, will be frowned upon by traditionalists. It's like an Italian eating a British Carbonara; it tastes fine, but it's not a Carbonara. Or as Chef Gino D'Acampo aptly put it in one of the British shows when he was told that if he added peas to his Carbonara it would be a British one, "If my Grandmother had wheels, she'd be a bike".

Semolina Crusted Fish

Semolina-crusted fish

Ingredients (serves 4-6):

- 500 g Fish fillets (firm-fleshed fish like tilapia, mackerel, kingfish, amberjack, halibut or trout work best, but softer fish-like haddock or cod can also be used)
- ¼ tsp Turmeric powder
- ½- 1 tsp Salt
- 1 tsp Kashmiri Chilli powder
- Juice of ½ lime (optional)
- Approximately 1 cup of Semolina

- 2 Tbsp Cornflour

- 3 Tbsp Oil

Method:

1. Wash the fish and pat it dry with a paper towel.

2. Add the fish, salt, chilli powder and turmeric to a mixing bowl and mix using your hands to ensure the fish is well coated. Cover and place in the fridge for an hour.

3. Mix the semolina and corn flour together and spread them as a thick layer on a flat tray or plate.

4. Remove the fish from the fridge, add the lime juice (if using) and give it a mix to coat.

5. Take one fillet of fish and press down lightly into the semolina-corn flour mixture. Turn it over and repeat to ensure the fish is properly coated. Repeat for each fillet.

6. Place the frying pan with oil on high heat and wait for the oil to heat up. The oil will start to shimmer when it's hot enough. Don't let the oil smoke.

7. Gently drop the coated fillets into the hot oil and let them fry for about 2 minutes on each side (for about ¾ inch thick fillets).

8. Take the pan off the stove and set it on a wire rack until ready to serve.

Recheado Masala - Whole Ingredients

This is one of the most versatile masalas in Goan cuisine and is the base for at least three curries and multiple preparations of fish. It's akin to an Indonesian 'sambal' and can be modified to use as a condiment. In fact, the hot sauce we served at my restaurant was a version of this masala.

Specific Equipment:

Mixer-grinder or food processor

Ingredients:

- 12 Kashmiri Red chillies
- 1 inch Ginger
- 8 cloves of Garlic
- 1 inch Cinnamon stick
- ¼ tsp Cumin
- 2 whole Cloves
- ½ cup Vinegar (Coconut or Apple Cider)
- ½ tsp Turmeric powder
- 1 tsp Black Peppercorns (3 g)
- 1 tsp Tamarind paste (10 g)
- 1 tsp Salt
- 2 tsp Sugar

Method:

1. Place all ingredients except for the vinegar into a blender jar and pulse a few times.

2. Add a splash of vinegar and grind to a fine paste. You may need to add more vinegar to lubricate the grind.

3. The paste should be ground smooth with no seeds or lumps.

4. You can store this paste for as long as you need. The vinegar pickles and preserves the other ingredients so it's virtually spoil-proof.

Recheado Masala - Ground/Powdered Ingredients

Ingredients:

- 15 g Kashmiri Chilli powder
- 5 g granulated Garlic
- 2 g Ginger powder
- 2 g ground Cinnamon
- 0.2 g ground Cloves
- 1.5 g ground Black Pepper
- 1 g ground Cumin
- 1 tsp Salt
- ¼ tsp Turmeric powder
- 75 ml (⅓ cup) Vinegar (Coconut or Apple Cider)
- 2 tsp Sugar

Method:

1. Mix all the dry ingredients together using a whisk.

2. Add in the vinegar and stir to remove all lumps.

3. Store in an airtight bottle and let it sit at room temperature for 3 days before using.

Recheado Fish

Recheado Fish

The word *recheado* in Portuguese means stuffed. *Recheado* fish is basically a stuffed fish, in this case, with *recheado* masala. This requires knife skills and the ability to butcher a fish (if the fish has not been gutted).

Ingredients (serves 1-2):

- 1 whole Mackerel (or any other whole fish with a strong flavour like bass, bream or tilapia)
- 2-4 Tbsp *Recheado* Masala (depending on the size of the fish)
- Salt to taste
- ¼-½ tsp Sugar (optional)
- 3-4 Tbsp Oil

Method:

1. Mix the sugar (if using) with the *recheado* masala.

2. Gut the fish by making a slit in the stomach from the vent up to the gills and then pulling out the entrails. Discard the entrails. Omit this step if your fish is already gutted.

3. On the dorsal side of the fish, locate the dorsal fins and bones. Using a sharp filleting knife, make a slit a few millimeters above the dorsal bone. Use long, sure strokes when cutting and stay as close to the central bones as possible. The slit should go almost all the way through to the stomach side, but not breach it.

4. Make a similar slit a few millimeters below the dorsal bone.

5. Stuff the two slits with the *recheado* masala and add some into the stomach cavity.

6. Season the fish with salt.

7. Place the frying pan with oil on high heat and wait for the oil to heat up. The oil will start to shimmer when it's hot enough. Don't let the oil smoke.

8. Add the fish gently to the pan.

9. Cook for about 3 minutes on each side to get a crispy skin and a flaky inside.

Bharilo Bangdo (Stuffed Mackerel)

This is another version of stuffed mackerel. In this case, the mackerel is stuffed with a green masala paste. This is usually made in Hindu households, but it is well enjoyed by everyone.

Specific Equipment:

Mixer-grinder or food processor

Ingredients (serves 2):

For the stuffing:

- 3 Thai Green Chillies
- 3 tablespoons grated Coconut
- 4-5 cloves of Garlic
- ½ inch Ginger
- 1 tsp Tamarind paste
- 1 tsp Coriander Seeds
- 4-5 Black Peppercorns

- ½ tsp Cumin
- 4 Tbsp chopped Coriander Leaves
- ½ medium-sized Onions, finely chopped

For the frying:

- 2 whole Mackerel, gutted and slit (method is described in the *Recheado* Fish recipe above)
- 1 tsp Salt or to taste
- ½ tsp Kashmiri Chilli powder
- ¼ tsp Turmeric powder
- 3 Tbsp Oil

Method:

1. Coat the mackerels with salt, chilli powder and turmeric powder, and set aside.

2. Put all the stuffing ingredients into a grinder/food processor, add 2 Tbsp water and blend into a smooth paste (add more water if required to get the consistency right).

3. Stuff the two slits of the mackerel with the paste and add some into the stomach cavity.

4. Place the frying pan with oil on high heat and wait for the oil to heat up. The oil will start to shimmer when it's hot enough. Don't let the oil smoke.

5. Add the fish gently to the pan.

6. Cook for about 3 minutes on each side to get a crispy skin and a flaky inside.

Masala Fried Shrimp/Prawns

Ingredients (serves 4):

- 500 g Shrimp/Prawns, peeled and deveined
- 3-4 tsp *Recheado* Masala
- 1 tsp Sugar
- 1 small Onion, finely diced
- ½ tsp Salt or to taste
- ¼ tsp Turmeric powder
- 2+1 Tbsp Oil

Method:

1. Sprinkle the salt, turmeric and 1 tsp of the *recheado* Masala over the shrimp/prawns and mix to coat.
2. Set aside in the fridge for about an hour.
3. Place a large frying pan on medium-high heat and pour 2-3 Tbsp of oil into it.
4. When the oil is hot, put the shrimp/prawns in, one at a time and cook them for about a minute on each side, until they get some colour.
5. Remove the shrimp/prawns from the pan and lower the heat to medium-low.

6. Add the remaining oil (if needed) and put the diced onion into the pan.

7. Sauté the onion until it starts to caramelize.

8. Add the remaining *recheado* masala and sugar (if using) and stir fry until it starts to caramelize.

9. Now add the shrimp/prawns back in and stir to coat.

10. Once the shrimp/prawns have heated through, remove from the heat and serve with your meal or as a snack.

In-Betweeners

Indians in general and Goans in particular are known for snacking in between meals, whether it's the mid-morning rice porridge known as *pez* or *kanji*, the infinite cups of tea consumed throughout the day, the evening tea time snacks, the "with drinks" snacks, or the post-drinking, pre-dinner snacks. One must note that not all of these are consumed every day. Well, except for the tea. Tea is Goa's coffee – consumed all day, every day.

Now, a popular misnomer used in the West for Indian styles tea is "chai tea". This term irks every self-respecting Indian as the word *chai* means "tea" in Hindi and some other Indian languages. In general, tea in India is made with just tea leaves, water and optionally, milk. So, when a person says "chai tea", they are essentially saying "tea tea". What is served in Starbucks when you order a "chai tea" or "chai latte" is what we would call a 'masala chai', which translates to "spiced tea".

Pallea Chao (Goan Black Tea)

Specific Equipment:

Strainer

Ingredients (serves 1):

- 1 cup of Water
- 1 tsp loose-leaf Tea
- Sugar as desired

Method:

1. Pour the water into a saucepan and bring it to a boil over medium heat.

2. Once the water is at a rolling boil, reduce the heat to low and add the tea leaves.

3. Let the water simmer with the tea leaves for about 3 minutes, and then turn off the heat.

4. Strain the tea into a cup.

5. Add sugar as desired and enjoy.

Chao (Milk Tea)

Specific Equipment:

Strainer

Ingredients (serves 1):

- ½ cup Water
- ½ cup Milk
- 1 tsp loose-leaf Tea
- 1 inch Ginger (optional)
- 2 pods Cardamom (optional)
- Sugar as desired

Method:

1. Pour the milk and water into a saucepan and bring them to a boil over medium heat.

2. Once the mixture is at a rolling boil, reduce the heat to low and add in the tea leaves and the ginger or cardamom (if using).

3. Let the tea simmer for about 3 minutes, then turn off the heat.

4. Strain the tea into a cup.

5. Add sugar as desired and enjoy.

Masala Chai

Specific Equipment:

Strainer

Ingredients (serves 2):

- 1 cup of Water
- 1 cup Milk
- 1 tsp loose-leaf Tea
- 2 pods Green Cardamom
- 1 inch Ginger
- 1 pod Black Cardamom
- 1 tsp Black Peppercorns
- 1 inch Cinnamon stick
- 1 flower Star Anise
- 3 whole Cloves
- Sugar as desired

Method:

1. Pour the milk and water into a saucepan and bring them to a boil over medium heat.

2. Once the mixture is at a rolling boil, reduce the heat to low and add the rest of the ingredients except sugar.

3. Let the mixture simmer for about 6 minutes, then turn off the heat.

4. Strain the tea into a cup.

5. Add sugar as desired and enjoy.

Notes:

Tea can be consumed at any time of the day. It's always served hot, irrespective of the outside temperature. Of course, with globalization, iced tea has been introduced and is quite popular, but traditionally, tea was always hot. Tea is often accompanied by some assorted fried snacks, especially in the evening. In fact, when I was a kid, the snack vendors all emerged in the evening.

Mirchi Bhoji & Kanda Bhoji

Mirchi Bhoji and Vegetable Pakoras, including Kaapa

Specific Equipment:

Deep fryer or a deep pot

Ingredients (serves 2-3):

- 1 cup of Chickpea Flour
- 1 cup of Water
- 2 Tbsp Rice Flour
- 1 tsp Baking Powder
- ½ tsp Salt
- 1 tsp Oregano Seeds or Celery Seeds or Cumin (optional)
- 3-4 Jalapenos or Hungarian Hot Chilli Peppers
- 1 Potato sliced into ⅛ inch rounds
- 1 cup of any other Vegetable you like. I recommend chopped cauliflower, chopped broccoli, green beans, snow peas, sliced eggplant or sliced zucchini.
- 4 cups Oil
- 2 Tbsp Salt dissolved in 2 cups of Water (Brine)

Method:

1. Make a slit along the length of the peppers without splitting them. If you're not a fan of heat, de-seed the peppers as well. Personally, I like to leave the seeds in.

2. Place the slit peppers, potato and other vegetables you're using into the brine solution and let them soak for between 1-4 hours.

3. In a mixing bowl, combine the chickpea flour, rice flour, salt, baking powder, oregano/celery seeds/cumin (if using) and water to form a thick paste. It should have the same consistency as pancake batter.

4. In the deep fryer or deep pot, heat the oil until it reaches a temperature of about 350°F (175 °C).

5. Drain the vegetables and place them on a kitchen towel to dry.

6. Take each piece, dip it into the batter to coat and then drop it into the hot oil.

7. Fry for 3-5 minutes until golden brown.

8. Serve with ketchup, tamarind sauce or mint and coriander chutney.

Goan Bhojis (Onion Pakoras)

Specific Equipment:

Deep fryer or a deep pot

Ingredients (serves 2-3):

- 1 cup of Chickpea Flour
- 1 cup of Water
- 2 Tbsp Rice Flour
- 1 tsp Baking Powder
- 1 tsp Salt
- 1 tsp Oregano Seeds, or Celery Seeds, or Cumin (optional)
- 2 Onions diced
- ¼ cup Coriander Leaves, minced
- 4 cups Oil

Method:

1. In a mixing bowl, combine the chickpea flour, rice flour, salt, baking powder, oregano/celery seeds/cumin (if using) and water to form a thick paste. It should have the same consistency as pancake batter.

2. Add the diced onions and minced coriander to the batter and mix until evenly distributed.

3. In a deep fryer or deep pot, heat oil until it reaches a temperature of about 350°F (175°C).

4. Using a teaspoon, scoop some of the mixture and drop it into the hot oil.

5. Repeat step 4 until you run out of batter (depending on the size of your deep fryer/pot, you may have to fry them in batches).

6. Fry for 3-5 minutes until golden brown.

7. Serve with ketchup, tamarind sauce or mint and coriander chutney.

Goan Vegetable Samosa and Vada Pao

Vada Pao – photo credit Samdhal

Specific Equipment:

Large saucepan with lid

Deep fryer or a deep pot

Ingredients (10-12 samosas):

- 3-5 large Russet Potatoes, peeled and diced into 1 inch cubes
- 1 Tbsp Mustard seeds
- 2 Tbsp + 1 l Oil
- 2 Onions diced
- 2 sprigs of Curry Leaves (optional)
- 2 slit Thai Green Chillies (optional)
- 1 tsp Cumin Seeds
- 1 tsp Coriander Seeds
- 2-3 Fenugreek Seeds
- ½ tsp Turmeric powder
- 1 cup of Water or as needed
- ½-1 tsp Salt
- 5 cloves of Garlic, minced
- 1 inch Ginger minced

For the samosas:

- 5-12 Large Wonton Wrappers

For the vada pao:

- 1 cup of Chickpea Flour
- 1 cup of Water
- 2 Tbsp Rice Flour
- 1 tsp Baking Powder
- ½ tsp Salt
- 1 tsp Oregano Seeds or Celery Seeds, or Cumin (optional)
- 10-12 Goan Pao or Ciabatta Buns

Method:

The filling:

1. Pour 2 Tbsp of oil into the saucepan and place it on medium-high heat.
2. Drop the mustard seeds into the pan and wait for them to start popping.
3. When they start popping, place the lid on and wait for the popping to stop.
4. Add the cumin, coriander seeds, fenugreek seeds, and curry leaves into the pan and fry them for about a minute.
5. Add the ginger and garlic, and sauté until fragrant.
6. Add in the onions (and chillies, if using) and sauté until they start to caramelize.
7. Add the potatoes and stir to coat with the oil.

8. Add the salt and water, and cover.

9. Cook until the potatoes are tender and the water is absorbed.

10. Lightly mash the potatoes to form a lumpy mixture.

11. (Only for vadas) Let the mixture cool down and then roll into golf ball-sized spheres.

12. (Only for vadas) Place the spheres uncovered in the refrigerator for 3-8 hours so that the outside dries a little.

Samosa - the wrapping:

1. Make a paste of a teaspoon of all-purpose flour and a little water.

2. Take a wonton wrapper and fold or cut it to form a long rectangle (about 3 inch wide and 8 inch long). Folding it will give you more crust, while cutting it won't.

3. Fold one end into a hollow cone, sealing the edge using a little flour paste.

4. Stuff about a tablespoon of the filling into the cone, fold the rest of the wonton wrapper around the cone to form a triangle.

5. Seal the end of the wonton wrapper using a little flour paste.

Vadas - the batter:

1. Combine the chickpea flour, salt, rice flour, baking powder and oregano/celery seeds or cumin (if using) in a mixing bowl using a whisk.

2. Add in the water and stir to create a thick batter.

Samosa - the final fry:

1. Heat the rest of the oil in the deep fryer or a deep pot to 350°F (175°C).

2. Drop the samosa into the oil and fry until golden brown.

3. Drain on a wire rack and serve with ketchup, tamarind sauce or mint-coriander chutney.

Vadas - the final fry

1. Heat the rest of the oil in the deep fryer or a deep pot to 350°F (175°C).

2. Take each potato ball, dip it into the chickpea batter to coat and then gently drop it into the hot oil. (Drop only a few vadas at a time so that the temperature of the oil doesn't fall below 330°F.)

3. Fry them until they are golden brown, then remove and drain on a wire rack.

Vada - the assembly

1. Cut a ciabatta bun through 3 sides, leaving the last side to form a kind of hinge at one end.

2. Smear one side of the bun with coriander-mint chutney.

3. Place a vada on the chutney, top it with garlic chutney and close the hinge to smash the vada.

4. Serve as a sandwich with more chutney on the side if desired.

Goan Beef Samosa

Specific Equipment:

Large saucepan with lid

Deep fryer or a deep pot

Ingredients (10-12 samosas):

- 500 g ground Beef
- 1 red Onion, diced fine
- 1 Shallot diced fine
- 5 cloves of Garlic, minced
- 1 inch Ginger root minced
- 1 tsp Cumin powder
- 1 Tbsp Coriander powder
- 2.5 g Cinnamon powder
- 1 tsp ground Black Pepper
- ¼ tsp Turmeric powder
- ¼ cup Coriander Leaves chopped fine
- 2 Thai Green Chillies chopped fine (optional)

- 5-12 Large Wonton Wrappers
- 2 Tbsp + 4 cups Oil

Method:

1. Mix the ground beef with the ginger, garlic, salt and spices and set in the fridge for about an hour.

2. Heat 2 Tbsp oil in a pan over medium heat.

3. Add in the onions and shallots and sauté until they start to caramelize.

4. Add the chillies (if using).

5. Add in the ground beef and stir to break up any lumps.

6. Add water if necessary and stir-fry until all the ground beef is browned and cooked.

7. Sprinkle some chopped coriander over the ground beef and take it off the heat.

8. Follow the same method for wrapping and frying as documented in the vegetable samosa recipe above.

9. Serve with ketchup or mint-coriander chutney.

Coriander Mint Chutney

Specific Equipment:

Mixer-grinder or food processor

Ingredients:

- 1 cup Coriander Leaves
- ½ cup Mint Leaves
- 2 Thai Green Chillies
- 2 cloves of Garlic
- ½ inch Ginger
- 1 tsp Salt
- Juice of one Lime
- 3-4 Tbsp Water

Method:

1. Place the coriander, mint, chillies, ginger and garlic into your blender with the salt and lime juice.
2. Blend it to form a smooth paste. Add water as needed.
3. Store in the fridge for up to a week or freeze for up to 3 months.

White Coconut Chutney

Specific Equipment:

Mixer-grinder or food processor

Pan with lid

Ingredients:

For grinding:

- 1 cup fresh shredded Coconut
- 1 inch Ginger
- 4 cloves of Garlic
- 1 cup of Water
- 1 tsp Tamarind paste
- 1 tsp Salt

For tempering:

- 2 Tbsp Oil
- 1 Tbsp Mustard Seeds
- 1 sprig (10-12 leaves) Curry Leaves
- 2-3 Fenugreek Seeds
- 1 tsp Cumin (optional)

Method:

1. Put all the grinding ingredients into the grinder/food processor and grind into a smooth paste to the consistency of a Greek yogurt. Set aside in a bowl.
2. Bring the oil up to a medium-high heat in a small pan.
3. Add the mustard seeds to the pan and cover until they stop popping.
4. Add the fenugreek seeds, curry leaves and cumin and sauté for a minute.

5. Take off the heat and pour the hot oil into the blended mixture in the bowl.

6. Stir the mixture until all the ingredients are mixed well.

7. Store in the fridge for up to a week.

Sometimes tea is accompanied by a sweet snack. There are probably individual names for each of the recipes, but we referred to them collectively as *godshem,* which translates to sweetish.

Doce Bhaaji

Ingredients (serves 6-8):

- 1½ cups broken Wheat (cracked wheat or bulgur)
- 400 ml Coconut Cream
- ¼ cup Coconut Jaggery
- 4 pods Green Cardamom (or ½ tsp Cardamom powder)
- ¼ tsp Nutmeg powder
- ¼ tsp Salt
- 2 Tbsp Ghee
- Nuts, as desired to garnish

Method:

1. If using broken wheat, soak it in water for about 2 hours, then drain and dry it. If using bulgur, skip this step.

2. Put the wheat or bulgur into a pot with 200 ml of water over medium heat and bring to a boil.

3. Add in the cardamom pods and jaggery, and let it simmer on a low heat for about 15 minutes, stirring occasionally.

4. Add in the coconut cream, ghee, nuts and salt, and let it cook for another 10 minutes. Taste and adjust seasoning.

5. Turn off the heat and garnish with nutmeg and some more nuts (if desired).

6. Serve warm.

One of the tea-time favorites is *alle-belle*, which is a kind of rice crepe stuffed with a mixture of shredded young coconut and coconut jaggery. When assembled, they looked a bit like squid tubes, which is why they are also referred to as *mankiyo* (the Konkani word for squid).

Alle Belle

Specific Equipment:

Mixer-grinder or food processor

Pan with lid

Ingredients:

For the crepe:

- 1 cup Rice (use short grain rice like Jasmine or Calrose)
- ⅓ cup Water + more for soaking
- 1 tsp Salt
- 2 Tbsp Oil

For the filling:

- ¼ cup Coconut Jaggery
- 1 cup fresh shredded Coconut

Method:

The crepe batter:

1. Wash the rice in cold water until the water runs clear.
2. Soak the rice in water for 4 to 5 hours or overnight.
3. Drain the soaked rice and put it into the grinder/food processor.
4. Add a little water and grind. Do not add a lot of water, as it will hamper the rice from being ground fine.
5. Add more water as required, to grind to a smooth and fine batter.
6. Transfer the batter to a large bowl.
7. Add about 2 cups of water and mix to get a thin, flowing, runny, and watery consistency. The quantity of water to be added depends on the quality and the type of rice.
8. Add the salt and mix well.

The filling:

1. Mix the coconut and the coconut jaggery in a bowl until they're properly combined.

The crepe:

2. Heat a cast-iron pan or a non-stick pan on medium to medium-high heat.

3. Drizzle ½ teaspoon of oil.

4. Spread the oil all over with a spoon, a small piece of cotton kitchen napkin, or half of an onion.

5. Stir the batter in the bowl with a ladle.

6. Fill the ladle with the batter, and pour the batter into the pan and spread it around by tilting the pan.

7. Fill in any large gaps with a little more batter.

8. Cover with a lid and cook the crepe till the batter firms up. Don't brown it or flip it. The edges will lift up from the pan when it's cooked.

The stuffing:

1. Put a spoon full of the filling onto the crepe in a line through the centre.

2. Take one side of the crepe and fold it over the filling.

3. Roll it up to form a tight wrap.

4. Serve hot or warm.

The Quasi-Meals

I personally consider *pez* (also known as *kanji*) and soup quasi-meals. These were a part of Goan culture and were probably needed back when everyone did a whole lot of physical labour. Today, these have been mostly phased out of the daily routine.

Pez

Pez was a way to use up the previous day's leftovers. Before refrigeration became affordable, leftover cooked rice was stored by submerging it in cold water. I cannot comment on the science behind it, but it worked. This leftover rice was then reheated with water and cooked to form a starchy porridge of mushy rice. The porridge was seasoned with salt and eaten with either *attoilo kodi* (leftover curry condensed to almost a paste-like consistency by boiling it down) or, in its absence, spicy pickles or *parra*. *Pez* was also the preferred diet if one was unwell, as it's considered easy on the stomach. But in such situations, the side would be a non-spicy pickle like *tora shero* (brined sliced green mangoes) or *chempni* (brined whole green mangoes). Today, *pez* is almost exclusively made when someone is sick. The only other time (that I'm aware of) that Goans eat *pez*, is on Good Friday when they're abstaining from rich food.

Pez or Kanji

Ingredients (serves 2):

- 200 g (1 cup) of short-grained Brown Rice (use Matta rice or Kendra from your local Indian store for best results)
- 750 ml (3 cups) Water
- 8 g (1½ tsp) Salt

Method:

1. Wash the rice a couple of times to get rid of the husk and other dirt.
2. Place the washed and drained rice in a saucepan and add the water and salt.
3. Cover the saucepan and cook on low/medium heat until the rice reaches a slightly mushy consistency.
4. Serve with condensed curry (*attoilo kodi*), or a pickle, or *parra*.

Notes:

- You can use pre-cooked rice for this recipe. If using pre-cooked rice, use equal quantities of rice and water and cook over medium heat until the rice becomes almost mushy.
- This recipe can be made with any rice, but keep in mind that this is usually made from a starchy rice. Using

brown rice (especially heritage/heirloom varieties) gives it a nicer taste.

- While traditionally paired with Goan pickles, I've found that it also pairs well with the South Indian *podi* (a.k.a. gunpowder), curd chillies, garlic coconut chutney, and roasted dry fish/jerky.

Pez and kismoor, served with assorted pickles

Soup

Soup is still sometimes made and consumed in the evenings, but in much smaller quantities, or as a replacement for a meal.

The thought of my grandmother's soup still makes my mouth water, which is what made me come up with this recipe. The base soup is almost the same, but I've added a few twists that make it my own. I call it *Caldo Pez*.

Caldo Pez consists of the base chicken alphabet soup, served with a Goan satay sauce and a half-boiled egg.

Caldo Pez

Ingredients (serves 4):

For the soup:

- ½ cup Brown Rice (preferably Goan or Matta)
- ½ cup Alphabet Pasta or Macaroni
- 3 litres Chicken or Beef Stock (or 3 Stock cubes in 3 litres of Water)
- 200 g Shredded Chicken or Beef
- 2 Shallots, chopped fine
- 2 cloves of Garlic, minced
- 1 cup *Vouchi Bhaji* (Malabar Spinach, or use regular spinach, if unavailable), chiffonade
- 2 Bay Leaves
- 1 Tbsp Oil

For the satay sauce:

- 3 Tbsp Oil (use unflavoured oil like sunflower/canola/vegetable)
- 4 cloves of Garlic (finely chopped)
- 1 inch fresh Ginger (finely chopped)
- 1 Shallot
- 2 tsp Chilli Flakes
- 1 Tbsp Honey
- 1 whole Mackerel *Parra* fried, de-boned, and shredded
- 1 Soft Boiled Egg (6 minutes on the dot) (optional)

Method:

The soup:

1. Place a large saucepan on medium heat.
2. Pour in the oil and wait until it's heated.
3. Add in the bay leaves and the minced garlic.
4. Sauté until the garlic starts to brown.
5. Add in the shallots and sauté until they are translucent.
6. Add in the shredded beef/chicken and the rice.
7. Mix until the rice is well coated with the oil.
8. Add in the stock and cover until it comes to a boil.
9. Add in the pasta.
10. Cook until the pasta is done to the desired texture.

11. Add in the *vouchi bhaji* and cover after turning off the heat.

The satay sauce:

1. Pour the oil into a pan and place it on medium-high heat.
2. Once heated, add in the shallots and fry until they are translucent.
3. Add in the ginger and continue frying until it begins to brown.
4. Now add in the garlic and let it cook until it starts to brown.
5. Add in the chilli flakes and the *parra*.
6. Stir for a couple of minutes and then add the honey.
7. Stir for another 5 minutes until well combined.
8. Leave the sauce to cool. The sauce can be stored in the fridge for a couple of days.

Assembly:

1. Slice the egg in half and place it inside a bowl.
2. Pour in the soup until it almost covers the egg.
3. Serve the satay sauce on the side.
4. You can also garnish the soup with deep-fried garlic, crispy onions, chopped coriander, sliced onions, or pickled chillies.

Notes:

- I've not added salt into the broth because generally, when using stock or stock cubes, there is sufficient salt in those. However, if you find that the salt is not to your taste, feel free to add more at any point after the stock is poured in.

- For the soup, use thick rice. The best variety is the local Goan red rice. Use Basmati only as a last resort.

- While the half-boiled egg is optional, I recommend it as the egg yolk adds a nice creamy richness to the soup.

- If you don't have access to mackerel *parra*, you can use a combination of dry shrimp/prawns and *recheado* masala (see the **Parra Substitute** recipe below):

Parra Substitute (only for Caldo Pez)

Ingredients:

- 1 Tbsp *Recheado* Masala
- 100 g Dry Shrimp/Prawns
- ½ cup Vinegar (Coconut or Apple Cider)
- 1 tbsp oil

Method:

1. Soak the dry shrimp/prawns in the vinegar for an hour.

2. Drain out the vinegar.

3. Mix the shrimp/prawns with the *Recheado* Masala.

4. Place a pan on a medium-high flame and pour the oil in.

5. Once hot, add in the mixture and fry until the masala begins to caramalize.

Chapter 7:
The Tavern

The tavern is a Goan institution. Every village, town, or settlement has at least one. Unlike the rest of India, in Goa, drinking is not taboo. Social drinking is very prevalent (perhaps another cultural gift from the Portuguese). It's also perhaps why the rest of India views Goa and Goans as drunks.

The tavern is where the men go for their "boys time", and while the topics of the discourse remain the same as those during tea time, the language is much more flowery and the snacks, much spicier.

Goan Sausages being sun dried

The snacks at taverns consist of small plates like *choris* – the spicy Goan sausage which we took from the Portuguese and bastardized to be spicier, sourer and a different type of delicious (taking us back to the subject of "What's authentic?"), fried fish crumbed with semolina after being seasoned with either turmeric and chili or the more complicated *recheado* masala, or if you're into a little heavier fare, you can have chilli fry or *aad maas* (translates to meaty bones).

These snacks are the Goan version of 'tapas', and the drinking session, snacks and all, is called *kop*, which loosely translates to a glass or cup. Unlike the Spanish, our tapas are consumed at a more laid-back or *sussegado* pace. The *kop* at the tavern usually ends by 6 p.m. or 7 p.m., by which time the men have to get home for the next routine of the day. In Catholic families, this would mean the rosary is recited by the family. In other families, I guess you could stay out a little longer and have another drink before heading home for dinner.

Chilli Fry

Use any protein for this recipe. It's most commonly made with beef or pork, but there are variations with chicken, seafood, or anything left over. It's fast, it's easy, and it's delicious. This is one of the most common foods available to order in the tavern, and probably one of the most popular to have with drinks.

Ingredients (serves 4-6):

- 500 g Beef or any other protein of choice, diced into 1 inch cubes
- 4 cloves of Garlic, minced
- ½ inch Ginger, minced
- 2 medium Onions (or 3 shallots), julienned
- 1-2 Thai Green Chillies, slit vertically
- ¼ tsp Turmeric powder
- 1 tsp Cumin
- 1 + ½ tsp Salt
- 1 tsp ground Black Pepper
- Juice of 1 Lime
- 2 Tbsp Oil (or sausage fat)
- 1 Tomato, diced (optional)
- 1 Bell Pepper, julienned (optional)

Method:

1. Put the cubed meat into a bowl with the minced ginger, garlic, 1 tsp salt and lime juice.
2. Mix thoroughly and let it sit in the fridge for at least an hour.
3. Place a pan on medium-high heat and pour in the oil.

4. Once the oil is hot, add in the onions and the remaining salt, and sauté until the onions soften and start to caramelize.

5. Add in the cumin, turmeric and pepper, and sauté for a minute.

6. If using tomato and bell pepper, add them in and sauté until the tomatoes release their juice and the peppers are soft.

7. Add in the marinated beef, and sauté for a few minutes until the beef starts to release liquid.

8. Reduce the heat to medium-low and sauté until the beef is cooked through (internal temperature of 165°F).

9. Serve with *pao*, *poie*, or rice.

Channa Chaat

This is not the same as the *channa chaat* made by North Indians. To be fair, *channa chaat* isn't even the correct name for this dish. In fact, it has no name. In the tavern, when ordering it, you'd probably just call it *chonne*, which is the Konkani word for chickpeas. Every tavern makes this differently, and this recipe is the one that I like best.

Ingredients (serves 4):

- 1 cup Chickpeas, soaked for at least 8 hours

- 2 cups of Water

- 1 Tbsp Salt

- 1 Shallot, diced fine

- ¼ cup Coriander leaves, minced

- ½ Lime

- 1 Green Chilli, minced

- ½ tsp Red Chilli powder or Chilli Flakes

- ¼ tsp ground Black Pepper

- ¼ tsp Cumin powder

Method:

1. Strain the chickpeas, discarding the water in which they were soaking.

2. Add the chickpeas into a heavy-bottomed pot with the water and salt (make sure that the water is at least 1 inch higher than the level of the chickpeas in the pot).

3. Bring the pot to a boil and let it simmer for 30 minutes to an hour, until the chickpeas are soft enough to eat.

4. Strain the chickpeas.

5. Mix the shallot, chilli and all the spices in a bowl.

6. Add the chickpeas and squeeze in the lime juice.

7. Toss to combine.

8. Taste and adjust the seasoning to your liking.

9. Add the coriander leaves as a garnish and serve warm or cold, as a salad or a snack with drinks.

Chilli Cheese Toast

This is a more contemporary tavern snack. Goans weren't very big on the use of dairy in our cuisine, as dairy was mostly reserved for tea, for young children or for opulent desserts. Cheese, though available during Portuguese rule, was hard to come by in the early days post-independence (or annexation, depending on whom you speak to). But after India's Operation Flood in the 1970s, a program which focused on increasing dairy yield and improving the supply chain specific to dairy through the use of co-operatives, all dairy products became much more accessible. That's when dishes like these were invented.

Ingredients

- 4 slices of Bread, cut in diagonals
- 4 Tbsp softened Butter, for spreading
- 200 g shredded processed Cheese (use a mozzarella cheddar mix to get that cheese pull)
- 4 Thai Green Chillis, or similar

Method:

1. Pre-heat an oven to 350°F (175°C).
2. Mince the chillis as fine as possible (consider putting them into a food processor or grind to a paste using a mortar & pestle).

3. Mix the chillis into the softened butter and set aside for about half an hour to infuse.

4. Spread a thin layer of butter on the slices of bread.

5. Place the bread on a parchment-lined baking tray and top with shredded cheese.

6. Toast in the oven for about 5 minutes or until the bread is crunchy and the cheese has melted.

7. Enjoy with green chutney or mayonnaise.

Butter Garlic Shrimp/Prawns

This is a dish that is considered quintessentially Goan by the rest of India. In fact, there are even chips (or as the British call them, crisps) made with the flavour called "Goan butter-garlic". However, I believe this dish finds its roots in European cuisine — probably Spanish, Italian, or maybe even Portuguese.

Ingredients:

- 500 g Shrimp/Prawns, peeled and deveined

- 100 g Butter

- 1 Tbsp Oil (use any kind you like, olive oil tends to give an interesting flavour)

- 4-5 cloves of Garlic, finely minced

- 2 Green Chillis, sliced fine (optional)

- 1 tsp Salt (or to taste)

Method:

1. Season the shrimp/prawns with salt and let them sit for at least half an hour.

2. Place a skillet or pan over medium-low heat and add the oil and butter.

3. Once the butter begins to foam, add in the garlic and chilli (if using) and stir for about 2 minutes.

4. Once the aroma of garlic changes from pungent to almost sweet and nutty, add in the shrimp/prawns.

5. Stir and let the shrimp/prawns cook for about 3 minutes on each side, basting with the garlic-butter emulsion often.

6. Take off the heat and serve with bread or as is.

Note:

Butter garlic is one of the preferred cooking methods for any seafood. It works well with shrimp/prawns, lobster, mussels, oysters, fish, and even crabs.

Chapter 8:
Sunday Lunch

Ah, Sunday!

The significance of Sunday may be a little difficult for non-Goans (or maybe it's non-catholics) to appreciate. First of all, when I was growing up, Goa and most of India had a six-day work week, which meant that Sunday was the only day off. Even schools ran from Monday to Saturday. Secondly, and this was more true in the villages than the cities, Sunday was the only day on which animals were slaughtered, be it goats, pigs or cows. Given the lack of refrigeration back then, it was the only day on which these meats were available. Lastly, and this is applicable only to the Catholics, it's the Sabbath. While God allegedly commanded that we were to rest on the 7th day, we Goans interpreted it as a call to CELEBRATE.

The day would begin with the ritual affirmation of our faith and spiritual identity (read as Sunday Mass). To the casual observer, it would appear to be a grand procession, a pageant even. Imagine a crowd, 300 strong, all dressed in their finest clothes, walking along the road to the church. It was quite the scene.

After the church service, we'd head straight to the bustling *bazaar* (local market) to hand-pick farm-fresh ingredients for lunch. Sunday lunch was a BIG THING! A traditional Sunday lunch almost always involved the participation of at least two non-pescatarian animals in addition to the usual fish and rice. This legendary three-in-the-afternoon fest was usually cooked from scratch with the women of the family labouring tirelessly over the fire while the men handled the butchering, indulging in their favourite drink.

Sunday lunch consisted of an array of dishes all brought together by a central rice dish. The special rice dish for celebratory occasions (and yes, Sunday lunch is an occasion) is called *pulao* (a bastardization of the Persian 'pilaf' or maybe the Arabic 'plov'), cooked with premium Basmati rice, infused with a heady mix of fragrant spices, flavoured with either chicken stock or fresh seafood, and finally tinted yellow with turmeric — probably a nod to the use of saffron by the revered Portuguese overlords.

The use of Basmati rice was especially significant, as this rice was expensive and difficult to procure. There were times when you couldn't get it, and the alternates would make the *pulao* less fragrant and hence not as tasty. The solution was to add "Basmati leaves" to the rice when cooking. "Basmati leaves" have nothing to do with the rice plant and were so called because of the fragrance akin to Basmati rice. In actuality, they are nothing but screw pine leaves (a.k.a. pandan leaves). Today, Basmati rice isn't hard to come by, nor is it as expensive as it was back then. And while this is good, it has resulted in the extinction of the use of the "Basmati leaves" in Goa.

Pulao

Ingredients (serves 2):

- 200 g (1 cup) Basmati Rice
- 400 ml (1¾ cups) Chicken or Vegetable Stock
- 1 medium Onion, diced
- ½ tsp Turmeric powder
- 1 Tbsp Oil
- 1 Bay Leaf
- 1 inch Cinnamon stick (2.5 g)
- 3 whole Cloves
- 1 pod Cardamom
- 1 tsp Black Peppercorns
- 2 petals of Star Anise
- Salt to taste

Method:

1. Wash the rice under running water until the water runs clear. (This is a key step to ensure you have light, fluffy rice. Washing the rice removes the loose starch, which prevents the grains from clumping together after cooking.)

2. Drain and set the rice aside.

3. In a saucepan, pour in the oil and place it over a medium heat.

4. Add in the bay leaf and all other whole spices. This will allow the flavours to infuse into the oil.

5. Add in the onions, a pinch of salt and the turmeric, and sauté until the onions are translucent.

6. Add the rice and stir until the grains are coated with the oil.

7. Pour in the stock and let the pot come to a boil.

8. Cover the pot and check every 10 minutes until the water has dried up. Do not stir the rice as this will release starch, which will make it sticky.

9. Once all the water is absorbed, take the pan off the heat and fluff it up gently using a fork.

Notes:

The above is the plain classic *pulao* recipe, which is inherently flavourful by itself and goes well with anything. However, there are different *pulao* that can be made by adding extra ingredients. The most popular are *tisreo* (clam) *pulao*, vegetable *pulao* and *choris* (Goan sausage) *pulao*. These versions elevate the dish even further, adding unique textures and rich flavours that complement the base *pulao* beautifully. Each variation brings its own cultural touch and delicious twist to this already versatile dish.

- For *tisreo* (clam) *pulao*, you'll need ¼ cup of steamed clams (without the shells) and 400 ml of clam juice. Cook the *pulao* using the clam juice instead of the stock, and stir in the clams towards the end of the cook (when the clam juice is 70% absorbed by the rice).

- For vegetable *pulao*, you'll need ¼ cup (in total) of a mix of diced carrots, chopped French beans and peas. Add these with the onions in step 5 of the recipe.

- For *choris* (Goan sausage) *pulao*, you will need about 250 g of Goan sausage in addition to the other ingredients. These need to be introduced with the onions in step 5 of the recipe.

Goan Roast Chicken

Roasting is one of the two ways in which chicken is prepared for Sunday lunch. The other is as a curry called *jeerem-meerem*, which contains more or less the same spices but includes an onion-tomato base.

Specific Equipment:

Mixer grinder or food processor

Ingredients (serves 5-6):

- 1 whole Chicken (fryer size is ideal, about 1-1.25 Kg)
- 1 head of Garlic (8 cloves)
- 2 inches Ginger

- 1 tsp Black Peppercorns
- 1 tsp Cumin
- 1 Green Chilli
- 1 inch Cinnamon stick (or ¼ tsp Cinnamon powder)
- 2 whole Cloves
- 1½ tsp Salt
- Juice of 2 Limes

Method:

1. Remove the chicken skin and set it aside for making stock or any other use you may have for it.
2. Grind all the remaining ingredients together into a fine paste using a food processor.
3. Apply the paste to the chicken, inside and out.
4. Leave the chicken to marinate in the fridge for 3-12 hours.
5. Remove the chicken from the fridge and let it come to room temperature (2 hours approximately).

If using an oven:

6. Preheat the oven to 350°F (150°C).
7. Place the chicken on a roasting pan, pour the marinade on the chicken, and set it on the middle rack of the oven.
8. Let it cook for 1 hour (or until an internal temperature of 170°F/75°C is reached in the thickest part).

9. Remove from the oven and let it rest for about 15 minutes before carving.

10. Pour the pan drippings into the serving platter and place the carved chicken on the drippings.

If using a stove top:

6. Slice up an onion and place it on the bottom of a heavy-bottomed pan.

7. Place the chicken and all the marinade into the same pan.

8. Add water to cover the bottom ½ inch of the pan.

9. Cover and place on low heat for about half an hour, turning halfway through.

10. Check that an internal temperature of 170°F is reached in the thickest part before taking it off the heat.

Jeerem-Meerem Chicken Curry

Specific Equipment:

Mixer grinder or food processor

Ingredients (serves 5-6):

- 1 whole Chicken (fryer size is ideal, about 1-1.25 Kg)

For the Masala:

- 1 head of Garlic (8 cloves)

- 2 inches Ginger

- 1 tsp Black Peppercorns

- 1 tsp Cumin

- 1 Green Chilli

- 1 inch Cinnamon stick (or ¼ tsp Cinnamon powder)

- 2 whole Cloves

- 1½ tsp Salt

For the curry:

- 2 large Onions, diced fine

- 4 Tomatoes, diced

- 1 tsp Tamarind paste (or 1 Tbsp Tamarind soaked in warm water)

- 1 Tbsp Oil

- 1-2 cups Water (as per desired thickness)

Method

1. Remove the chicken skin and set it aside for making stock or any other use you may have for it.

2. Cut the chicken into small pieces. Generally, for Indian curries, we do what is called a curry cut, which involves breaking the chicken down into 8 pieces as is normally done, and then cutting the breast, thighs and legs into smaller parts by cutting through the bone. If you don't have a cleaver, you can leave it at the 8 pieces, or alternatively, you can use boneless chicken diced into cubes; however, the bones are where the flavour's at and keeping them in the curry will make it that much better.

3. Grind the ingredients for the masala into a paste using the mixer/grinder or food processor.

4. Apply this paste to the chicken and leave it to marinate for 1 hour up to overnight in the fridge.

5. Place a large pot over medium-high heat.

6. Pour in the oil, and once it comes to temperature, add in the onions.

7. Sauté the onions until they soften and start to caramelize.

8. Add in the tomatoes and let them soften. Keep cooking the tomatoes until the fat begins to separate from the water.

9. Now add the marinated chicken along with all the masala.

10. Pour the two cups of water into the bowl used for marinating to capture any remnants of the masala.

11. Add the water to the pot and lower the heat to medium.

12. Bring the curry to a boil, and then add in the tamarind paste or strained tamarind water.

13. Let it simmer for about 10 minutes before tasting and adjust the seasoning to your taste.

14. Boil the curry down to your desired consistency and then turn off the heat.

15. Serve with rice, *pulao* or bread.

Caldinho - Traditional

This is a very mild (in terms of heat) but flavourful curry that I find really showcases the core ingredient of the curry, be it fish, vegetable or meat.

Caldinho is a Portuguese word that translates literally into small soup, and in my restaurant, I have served this curry as a vegan pumpkin or squash soup. However, in Goan cuisine, it is a curry and is usually eaten over rice or with bread. It's one of the curries usually made on special occasions, including Sundays.

Specific Equipment:

Mixer-grinder or food processor

Ingredients (serves 4-6):

For the spice paste (masala):
- ½ cup shredded/grated Coconut
- 6 cloves of Garlic
- ½ inch Ginger (½ Tbsp Ginger paste)
- ¼ tsp Turmeric powder
- 1 Tbsp Coriander seeds
- 1 tsp Cumin
- 1 tsp Black Peppercorns

For the fond:

- 2 Onions, diced

- 2 Thai Green Chillies (optional)

- 2 Tbsp Oil

For the poaching:

- 500 g Fish, cut into steaks (the best fish for caldinho is pomfret, but amberjack or shrimp/prawns work really well too)

- 1 tsp of Tamarind paste

- A few Coriander Leaves chopped for the final garnish

- Salt to taste

Method:

1. Pour 2 Tbsp of hot water over the tamarind in a bowl and leave to soak.

2. Place all the masala ingredients into the blender with a few Tbsp of water and blend to a smooth paste.

3. Pour the blended paste through a sieve and into a container to extract a flavoured coconut milk.

4. Put the contents of the strainer back into the blender with about ½ cup of water and blend again.

5. Strain the blended paste into the same container as the first extract.

6. Repeat steps 4 & 5 one more time before discarding the contents of the strainer. You should end up with about 1.5-2 cups of flavoured coconut milk extract.

7. Wash the fish, pat dry with a paper towel and season with ½ to 1 tsp salt.

8. In a pot/saucepan, heat the oil to a medium-high temperature.

9. Add in the onions and sauté them for a few minutes.

10. Once the onions are soft and start to caramelize, add in the chillies (if using) and pour in the flavoured coconut milk extract from step 6.

11. Bring the curry to a boil and then reduce the heat to low.

12. Add in the fish, one piece at a time and cover. Once the fish is added, do not stir using a spoon, as that can cause the pieces of fish to break apart. Instead, shake the entire saucepan/pot gently in circular motions to stir.

13. Wring out all the juices of the tamarind into the water it was soaking in. Discard the wrung tamarind and pour some of the tamarind water into the pot.

14. After about 10 minutes, taste the curry and adjust the seasoning with salt and tamarind water.

15. Let it boil for 5 more minutes and then turn off the heat.

16. Garnish with the chopped coriander leaves.

17. Serve over rice or *pulao*.

Notes:

- *Caldinho* is a very versatile curry and is an excellent one for vegans. While traditionally made with fleshy white fish with a mild sweet flavour, shrimp/prawns, and sweet vegetables like squash, turnips, kohlrabi, breadfruit or okra, you could even make it with white pumpkin (marrow), green papaya or sweet potatoes.

- You can even use a combination of main ingredients. A popular one we used, when I was young, was white pumpkin (marrow) or papaya and dry shrimp/prawns. Another common one was cauliflower and shrimp/prawns. And while typically made with fish or vegetables, I wouldn't be surprised if someone's tried making a chicken *caldinho*.

Caldinho - Easy Recipe

Ingredients (serves 4-6):

- 500 g Fish, cut into steaks (the best fish for caldinho is pomfret, but amberjack or shrimp/prawns work well too)

- 1 Tbsp ground Coriander

- 1 tsp ground Cumin

- 1 tsp ground Black Pepper

- ¼ tsp Turmeric powder

- 400 ml Coconut Cream

- 2 Thai Green Chillies

- 2 Onions, diced fine

- 5 cloves of Garlic, minced (1 Tbsp)

- ½ inch Ginger, minced (1½ tsp)

- 2 Tbsp Oil

- 1 tsp Tamarind paste

- ½-1 tsp Salt

Method:

1. Pour 2 Tbsp of hot water over the tamarind in a bowl and leave to soak.

2. Wash the fish, pat dry with a paper towel and season with ½ to 1 tsp salt.

3. In a pot/saucepan, heat the oil to a medium-high temperature.

4. Add in the onions, ginger, garlic and chillies and sauté until the onions begin to caramelize.

5. Add in the coconut cream and the spice powders.

6. Once the curry starts to boil, reduce the heat to medium-low and let it simmer.

7. Add in the fish and cover for about 15 minutes. Once the fish is added, do not stir using a spoon, as that can cause the pieces of fish to break apart. Instead, shake the entire saucepan/pot gently in circular motions to stir.

8. Wring out all the juices of the tamarind into the water it was soaking in. Discard the wrung tamarind and pour some of the tamarind water into the pot.

9. Taste the curry and adjust the seasoning with salt and tamarind water.

10. Let it boil for 5 more minutes and then turn off the heat.

11. Garnish with the chopped coriander leaves.

12. Serve over rice or *pulao*.

Vindaloo

Goan Pork Vindaloo/ Vindalho

Arguably, Goa's most famous export. The *vindaloo* or *vindalho* (as it's spelt by the remnants of the Portuguese sympathizers in the state) can be found on any Indian restaurant menu. It's one of the most popular items to order when Brits head out for their *Ruby Murray* (look up rhyming slang). In my experience, however, there are very few restaurants or curry houses that actually get the flavours right.

Vindaloo is one of those dishes that the colonizers (Portuguese) brought into India with them. It's name derives from the terms *vin* and *alho,* translating to wine and garlic, respectively. But when they brought it to Goa along with the chillis, we went ahead and spiced it up. Also, not having access to wine in Goa, we replaced the wine with coconut vinegar to create the fiery curry. Traditionally, *vindaloo* is only ever made with pork as the main ingredient, though with assimilation (or appropriation) it's now most popular with lamb outside Goa.

Specific Equipment:

Mixer-grinder

Ingredients:

For the curry paste:
- 10-12 dry Kashmiri Chillis (I usually mix in a few spicier chillis like Thai or Arbol, but that's optional)
- 10 cloves of Garlic
- 1½ inches Ginger
- 1 tsp Turmeric powder

- ½ tsp Cumin

- ½ tsp Black Peppercorns

- 1½ inches Cinnamon

- 4 Cloves

- ¼ cup Vinegar

- 1 Shallot

For the marination:

- 500 g Pork (pork shoulder or similar; the loin tends to dry out, but is still enjoyable), diced into 1 inch cubes

- 2 tsp Salt (or to taste)

- ¼ tsp Turmeric powder

For the base:

- 1 large Onion (about 250 g)

- 1 Tbsp Sugar (optional)

- 1 Tbsp Oil

- 250-500ml Water (depending on the consistency you want)

- 1 Tbsp Tamarind paste (optional)

- 2 Thai Green Chillies (optional), slit through

Method:

1. In a bowl, add the marination ingredients and mix to coat. Let this sit for at least an hour, to overnight in the fridge.

2. Put the curry paste ingredients into the mixer grinder and grind to a smooth paste. Add more vinegar when grinding, if required.

3. Place a saucepan over medium-high heat and add in the oil.

4. Once the pan has reached temperature, add in the onions and let them sweat.

5. Once the onions are softened and start to caramelize, add in the ground paste from step 2 and stir to combine.

6. Let the paste cook for about 2 minutes, stirring continuously to avoid burning.

7. Add in the water and stir to dissolve the paste.

8. Let the mixture come to a boil.

9. Bring the heat down to medium-low and add in the marinated pork.

10. Let the pork cook for about 15 minutes then taste and adjust seasoning. Add the sugar and tamarind paste in at this point, if using.

11. Add in the green chillies, if using.

12. Let it simmer for a further 15 minutes before turning off the heat.

13. Serve with *pao* or steamed rice.

PART 3:

SEASONS IN THE SUN

Chapter 9:
Summertime and the Eatin' is Easy

As kids growing up in Goa, we looked forward to the months of April and May. That was when most schools broke for the summer holidays—the only long holiday in the school year that did not include holiday homework. It was the only time of the year when we were truly allowed to do whatever we wanted. Before we proceed, I should warn you, I'm going to slip into one of those 80s/90s kids vs. today's kids clichéd rhetoric that you've probably heard a million times. And here it comes:

We really did leave the house in the morning, and aside from breaks for snacks, lunch and tea, we wouldn't return until we lost whatever ball we were playing with because it was too dark to find. We played largely unsupervised, with an occasional reprimand from a passing adult who happened to see us doing something we weren't supposed to be doing. We played in the streets or in whatever open space we could find. Yes, we broke a few window panes and roof tiles, and were scolded for it—sometimes by our own parents, sometimes by others, often both, but that's how we grew up. They say it takes a village, and we were raised by one.

117

Now that that's out of my system, let me tell you why summer holidays were so special for us. Summer was when you got the best fruits and the best entertainment, especially in small villages. Every week during summer, there'd be a new *tiatr* (folk plays filled with political satire, innuendo, slapstick comedy, soap opera-level drama, and of course, songs) performed.

The *tiatr* would take place in the church hall, unless it was booked for a wedding or some other party, in which case it would be held on the church football — not soccer, football the one played with your feet — ground (almost every village church in Goa has one on its property).

A makeshift stage would be erected, and tin roofing sheets would form the walls that enclosed the area that would seat paying customers. You had to admire the designers of these make-shift theatres because no matter what you did, if you weren't within the tin walls, you wouldn't be able to see the play. Even the small holes that adorned the tin sheets were masked with black cloth, and the walls were high enough that even the raised stage couldn't be seen.

We managed to watch a show for free just once, when a *tiatr* was staged under a large *gulmohar* (Royal Poinciana) tree. We climbed onto its branches and enjoyed the entire performance. We never did that again, though, because those trees bloom in summer, and the falling dew, sap, nectar, and flowers coated us and were extremely difficult to wash off.

The *tiatr*, though not unique to Goa, is uniquely Goan. It is, at its core, a play, usually modelled around Catholic culture and

118

life in the tiny state. It has all the elements usually expected of entertainment.

There's humor—albeit mostly slapstick, sometimes sexist, often racial, and even more frequently, body-shaming. There's drama—the kind one would expect from a Hindi *saas-bahu* (mother-in-law–daughter-in-law) soap opera, or, in a more international sense, from a K-drama or telenovela. There's suspense—the classic whodunit. And of course, there's the songs and musical interludes, often set to the tunes of contemporary popular Bollywood hits (we are, after all, Indian, and where would India be without its Bollywood beats). The lyrics to these songs were rewritten to insinuate criticism of local officials, politicians and policies, without outright naming and shaming—a prevalent art form in autocratic societies, which resulted in some of our best nursery rhymes.

It is an art, but not the snobbish kind you would see at a gallery, nor the kind where you sit in a cushioned seat with your gold-plated binoculars, giving hushed praises through pursed lips and muted applause. It's the kind where you get involved in the play to the extent that you might get out of your seat and dance because the villain is defeated, or just cause the rhythm got you, or you got it. The actors don't expect standing ovations, they don't expect praise for a pitch-perfect song, and they don't expect roses to be thrown at them. They judge their success by the involvement of the audience – the unabashed laughter at the jokes or antics, the collective gasp or sigh let out by the room when a plot twist is revealed or when the hero gets the girl, the wolf whistles and howls at the lyrics being sung. It does exactly what good art is supposed to do—it holds up a mirror to society and forces one to step into the looking glass, while being entertaining.

Attending a *tiatr* was usually either preceded or followed by snacks, if you could call them that, at our local street cart vendor. This was usually the quintessential *roce* omelette. If I were ever asked to put Goa on a plate, this would be my Goa. A simple meal consisting of an omelette, a *xacuti*-like gravy made with either chicken, mutton (goat), or beans, topped off with a sprinkle of chopped onions and coriander, served with a wedge of lime and bread – a choice of *poie, unde, katre pao,* or *pao kadak/moh.* This street fare is something you won't find anywhere else in India (to my knowledge at least), and it's delicious. As kids, this was the perfect pre-*tiatr* meal. And ever since we learned the secrets of alcohol, it became the perfect post-pubbing/clubbing/dance meal. During wedding season (the time between the monsoon and Lent), you'll find carts serving this deliciousness right into the wee hours of the morning, catering to drunks, party-goers, and most often musicians and other event-management staff who didn't have time to eat at the gig.

Roce Omelette

Roce Omlette

Ingredients (serves 1):

- 1 Egg
- 1 cup Xacuti Gravy
- 1 + 1 tsp Onions, diced
- ½ tsp Tomatoes, diced
- A pinch of Turmeric powder
- A pinch of Coriander powder
- A pinch of Cumin powder

- A pinch of Salt

- 1 wedge of Lime

- 1 Tbsp Oil

- A pinch of Coriander leaves, minced

- 1 *Pao* or other bread of your choice

Method:

1. Pour the oil into a pan and place the pan over medium-high heat.

2. In a glass or bowl, break in the egg, add 1 tsp of the onions, tomato, spice powders and salt, and beat it all together.

3. Pour the egg mixture into the hot pan and swirl it around to form a thin omelette.

4. Once the edges get a little crispy, flip the omelette over and cook the other side.

5. Once cooked completely, fold it into quarters, take it off the pan and place it on a plate.

6. Pour the warmed *xacuti* gravy over the omelette.

7. Mix the remaining onions with the coriander leaves and sprinkle them on top of the omelette.

8. Serve with a wedge of lime and bread.

While the classic street food that is the *roce omelette* is a great hangover food, I found myself wanting to refine it to make it more presentable for fine dining. That's how I came up with

Ilha do Sol (isle of the sun), as I call it. This dish leaves the gravy portion of the dish relatively untouched, but includes a meat protein, and the omelette is replaced with a sunny-side-up egg whose runny yolk just adds to the richness of the dish.

Ilha Do Sol

Ilha do Sol

Specific Equipment:

Mixer grinder or food processor

Cast-iron pan

Frying pan with lid

Ingredients (serves 2):

For the gravy:

- 7 Kashmiri Red Chillies
- 1 inch Cinnamon stick
- 2 petals of Star Anise
- 1 tsp Cumin seeds
- 1 tsp Turmeric powder
- 2 Tbsp Coriander seeds
- 1 Tbsp Black Peppercorns
- 2 petals of Mace
- 2 pods of Cardamom, crushed
- 1 Tbsp Poppy seeds
- 200g grated Coconut
- 5 cloves of Garlic
- 1 inch Ginger, peeled
- 2 Shallots
- 1 tsp Tamarind paste
- 200 ml Coconut Milk
- Salt to taste

For the proteins:

- 2 Filet Mignon Medallions or 200 g of Chicken

- 2 cloves of Garlic
- ¼ inch Ginger, peeled
- Salt and Pepper to taste
- 1 Tbsp + 1 tsp Oil
- 2 Eggs

Method:

The gravy:

1. In a pan over low heat, roast each of the following spices separately until they are aromatic: chillies, cinnamon, star anise, cumin, turmeric, coriander, pepper, mace, cardamom, and poppy seeds.

2. Place all the spices in the jar of a dry grinder and grind to a fine powder.

3. Set the powder aside.

4. Using the same pan over low heat, roast the coconut, ginger, garlic and shallots until they start to caramelize.

5. Place the roasted ingredients and tamarind into the grinder/food processor.

6. Pour about ½ to 1 cup of water, and grind into a wet paste.

7. Add the dry powder to the paste and stir to combine.

8. Place a heavy-bottomed pot over medium heat and pour the paste into the pot.

9. Bring the gravy to a boil, adding water as required.

10. Add the meat to the pot.

11. Cover the pot and let it come to a boil.

12. Simmer for about 15-20 minutes.

13. Place a saucepan on medium heat and pour 1 tsp of oil into it.

14. Add the paste into the saucepan and let it cook till the aroma of the paste is no longer pungent.

15. Add in the coconut milk and bring it to a boil.

16. Add salt to taste and let it simmer for about 10 minutes. Cover and set aside.

The meat and eggs:

1. Pat the meat (beef or chicken) dry.

2. Season with salt and pepper on both sides and set aside for about half an hour.

3. Grind the garlic and ginger together to form a paste.

4. Add this paste to the meat and massage it into the meat properly.

5. Let the meat marinate in the paste for about half an hour.

6. Place a cast-iron (preferably) pan on high heat and heat 1 Tbsp of the oil in it.

7. When the oil reaches the smoking point, gently place the meat into the pan.

8. Cook the meat for about 2 minutes on each side (it should be golden brown) before placing the pan into a

preheated oven at 200°C (400°F) for 20 minutes (30 minutes for chicken)

9. Remove the pan from the oven and let the meat rest.

10. Pour 1 tsp of oil into a frying pan (that has a lid) and place it over low heat.

11. Break the eggs into the frying pan, cover the pan, and let the eggs cook slowly for about 10 minutes.

12. When the white portion of the eggs is firm, you can remove the eggs from the pan.

Assembly:

1. Place a single medallion of beef (or half the quantity of chicken) in the centre of a shallow bowl.

2. Pour about 1 cup of the gravy over the meat.

3. Place the egg on top of the meat.

4. Serve with a wedge of lime and toasted bread on the side.

Summertime was also when most relatives who lived in other parts of India (or the world) came back to visit. Our ancestral homes were filled to the brim, and sleeping arrangements were interesting to say the least. I have no idea what the adults' arrangements were, but we kids all slept in the hall. The floor would be covered with a mixture of straw mats, cotton mattresses, rugs and quilts to create one large sleeping area. Fourteen of us, first, second and third cousins, once, twice or thrice removed, all shared this sleeping area. It was like camping and a great way to bond.

During these visits, the family would busy themselves in preparation for the upcoming monsoon season. We'd make pickles, sausages, vinegar, dried fish, and the like. The extra manpower made for lighter workloads, though, as is always the case with family, stress levels were through the roof. There was also the passive-aggressive one-upmanship between the homecoming nuclei, with each family trying to prove their financial success by spending money on things that weren't usually purchased. "Don't cook today, I'll get some snacks from the market.", "Don't worry, we'll go out for dinner tonight, my treat.", were common phrases heard. Of course, as kids, none of it bothered us. We'd get all we asked for and more. Needless to say, the local snack vendors selling loads of croquettes, patties, samosas, fish cutlets, etc. benefitted from the situation.

Fish Cutlets

Ingredients:

- Goan Style Poached Fish with all the gravy and onions (see next recipe)
- 1 slice of Bread (use stale bread if available)
- 1 Egg
- 1 cup Semolina
- 4 Tbsp Oil

Method:

1. Remove the fish from the poaching liquid and set aside.

2. Place the pot with the onions, garlic, spices and poaching liquid on low heat and bring to a boil. The aim is to reduce the liquid as much as possible.

3. Debone the fish and discard the bones.

4. Once the liquid is almost dried up, take the pot off the heat.

5. Remove and discard the whole spices as best as you can.

6. Add the deboned fish back into the pot and mash it all into a paste.

7. If the paste is too moist, tear up the bread and add it to the mixture. Combine it to form a drier paste with the consistency of uncooked meatballs.

8. Form the paste into a round patty as you would a fish cake or a burger patty.

9. Repeat until all the paste is used up.

10. Beat the egg thoroughly in a shallow bowl.

11. Dip each patty into the egg and then dredge it through the semolina until it is coated completely.

12. In a pan, heat the oil until it starts to shimmer.

13. Place the patties into the hot oil and fry until the semolina is golden brown (about 2 minutes on each side).

14. Serve as a snack or as a side with a meal.

Goan Style Poached Fish

Specific Equipment:

Saucepan or stock pot large enough to accommodate the fish

Ingredients (serves 3-4):

- 500 g Mackerel (or other fatty fish like salmon), gutted and kept whole
- 4-6 cloves of Garlic
- 1 Onion, sliced into rings
- 1 tsp Black Peppercorns
- 1 tsp Cumin
- 2 whole Cloves
- 1 inch Cinnamon stick
- 1 tsp Oil (optional)
- 1 Tomato, sliced (optional)
- ½ tsp Salt

Method:

1. Season the fish with salt on both sides and set aside for half an hour to an hour.
2. Pour the oil (if using) into the saucepan or stock pot and spread it to cover the base.

3. Arrange the sliced onion evenly to cover the base of the pan.

4. Add the garlic, tomatoes (if using) and all the whole spices.

5. Place the fish on top.

6. If not using oil, add a couple of tablespoons of water to the pan.

7. Cover the pan, place it over very low heat and let it cook undisturbed for an hour.

8. After an hour, open the lid and check if the fish is cooked properly (internal temperature of 140°F).

9. Serve the fish either with bread or with rice.

Beef Croquettes

Goan croquettes are different from the European ones. First of all, they're pronounced "crow-kays" (I've no idea why). And second, they don't use potatoes. Instead, it's just pot roast ground with Goan sausage, bread and eggs, formed into little cylinders, crumbed, and deep-fried.

Specific Equipment:

Mixer-grinder or food processor

Pressure cooker

Ingredients (makes 10-20 croquettes):

For the roast:

- 500 g Beef (in order of preference – blade roast, tri-tip, striploin – the fattier the better)
- 1 tsp Cumin
- 1 tsp Black Peppercorns
- 3 whole Cloves
- 1 inch Cinnamon stick
- ¼ tsp Turmeric powder
- 6-8 cloves of Garlic
- 1 inch Ginger
- 2 dried Red Chillies (any kind)
- 1 Lime
- 1 Onion
- 1 tsp Salt or as needed

For the grind:

- 2 slices of Bread
- 200 g Beef Fat (optional, but recommended)
- 50 g Goan Sausage (or Spicy Chorizo)
- 1 Egg

For breading:

- 1 cup Semolina (or as needed)

Method:

The roast:

1. Grind the cumin, peppercorns, cloves, cinnamon, turmeric, ginger, garlic and lime juice in the grinder/food processor. This paste is what we call roast masala.

2. Slice the onions and place them in the pressure cooker.

3. Coat the meat with the roast masala and salt, and add it to the pressure cooker.

4. Break the chillies and add them to the pressure cooker. Give everything a mix and let it marinate in the fridge overnight.

5. After about 8-12 hours, take the pressure cooker out of the fridge. Check how much liquid is in it. There should be at least an inch of liquid at the bottom. If there isn't enough, add some water to get it to that level.

6. Place the pressure cooker on low heat with the weight on.

7. Let the meat cook for an hour on low heat, and then take it off the heat and let the pressure release naturally.

The grind:

1. When the roast cools down, divide the beef into 5 portions.

2. Cut the fat into 5 portions.

3. Remove the sausage meat from the casing and divide the meat into 5 portions.

4. Insert the finest blade you have into the meat grinder and turn it on.

5. Feed one portion of meat, one portion of fat, one portion of sausage, some bread, some onions and spices from the pressure cooker to the meat grinder.

6. Repeat step 5 until you've finished grinding all the ingredients (including the onions and spices).

7. Add some of the liquid from the pressure cooker (it's not necessary to use all of the liquid), and combine by kneading or stirring. The mixture should be the consistency of raw meatballs.

8. Add in the egg and combine.

9. Scoop a small ball of the mixture into your hand and shape it into a small cylinder (about 2 inch long and ½ inch in diameter).

10. Repeat until you run out of the ground roast.

The breading:

1. In a flat tray, spread the semolina as a thin layer.

2. Take each cylinder of meat and roll it in the semolina to coat. It should coat easily, as the cylinders will still be moist.

3. Place the coated cylinders on a tray and set aside. You can freeze these for up to three months in sealed boxes and fry them as needed.

The frying:

1. If the croquettes are frozen, take them out of the freezer about 1 hour before frying.

2. In a deep fryer or deep pot, pour in the oil.

3. Heat the oil to 350°F (175°C).

4. Drop a few croquettes into the hot oil one at a time (if frying from frozen, drop a maximum of 3 so that the temperature of the oil doesn't drop too much).

5. Fry until golden brown on the outside, and leave to cool on a wire rack.

Fruits and Ferments

The beginning of the Goan summer means two things: mangoes and *urrack*. Goan summer officially starts in April, even though the temperatures start getting to you by mid-March. As Charles Dickens said (as you know by now, I'm paraphrasing), "these are the best of times, these are the worst of times." Temperatures soar during March to May, and with the humidity at about 90%, it's hot, sticky and exhausting.

Speaking of sticky, have you ever tried eating Goan summer fruits? Summer brings the best produce: cashews, jackfruit, mangosteen, Indian plums, and assorted wild berries.

The abundance of fruits is what makes the weather bearable. The pièce de résistance, however, is the mango. In Goa, mango season is talked about more than the weather. Well, actually, the weather is talked about in relation to the mangoes — or, to be precise, the effect it will have on the mango yield.

Months before the first signs of the fruit, small talk revolves around the "mango weather". "Oh no, there's so much dew these days, all our mango flowers will fall, and we won't have a good crop this year." "It looks like it might rain. I hope it doesn't, else we will get worms in the mangoes."

It's an obsession we go through every year. You'll hear theories from anyone who has a mango tree: "Don't water the tree at all," or "Make sure you water the tree when it flowers." Like everything else in Goa, everyone has an opinion.

India's most famous mango variety (Yes, there are different varieties of mangoes. Over 100 and counting.) is probably the *hapus* (alphonso mango), especially the ones grown along the Konkan coast between Ratnagiri and Malvan. In Goa, however, we rave about our two favourite varieties: the *malcurad*, also called *mancurad* depending on where in Goa you come from (a reminder about the changing dialects every 3 km) and the *musurad*. For the average Goan palate, anything other than these two does not qualify as a real mango. We'll eat it, enjoy it, but at the end, we'll always say, "nothing compared to our *malcurad/musurad*".

The *musurads* are juicier and have fewer fibres, and are usually used to make *mangada* (a mango jam). The *mancurads* are more fibrous, but taste much better and are eaten as dessert for the few months that they are available.

Another mentionable is the unripe mango, which is colloquially called "raw mango" because everyone knows that the opposite of ripe is raw. I guess it finds its roots in Indian languages, where the words for uncooked and unripe are the same: 'kachha'. The unripe mango is sour and is used in an array of pickles.

The most famous of the Goan mango pickles is probably *miscut,* green mango slit halfway through, its yet unformed seed discarded, stuffed with a spice paste and left to pickle in oil.

The next most popular pickle is what we call *chepni.* Here, green mangos whose seeds have not yet formed are salted and stacked in a bin with a heavy weight applied onto the mangos. Over the next few days, osmosis ensures that you have shriveled-up mangoes in a brine solution.

Another much loved mango pickle is one made with the unripe mangos that fall off the tree early. It's known by two names, *coromb* or *tora sheere,* the latter more commonly used in South Goa.

Tora Sheere

Tora sheere literally translates to "unripe mango" (*tor*) "slices" (*sheere*), and is sliced unripe mango soaked in brine.

All three of these pickles make great accompaniments for the other best part of the summer: *urrack*. It may seem like I'm teasing since I've now mentioned the word twice without a description. Bear with me, as this drink deserves a proper introduction.

For the uninitiated, Goa is quite famous for its local moonshine called *feni*. *Feni* is of two types: *coconut feni*, made from toddy (the sap of the coconut tree), and *cashew feni*, made from the juice of the cashew apple.

Cashew Apples (with the nuts removed) ready for juicing

Traditionally, your preference depended on your region of origin: cashew for the North Goans, coconut for the South Goans. Today, the coconut version appears to be going extinct, like most other recipes of the South.

The exact origin of this alcoholic drink is unknown. Some say that the evil Portuguese brought fermentation and distillation know-how with them, corrupting the innocent Goans by exposing them to the consumption of inebriating drinks, rendering them alcoholics and thus unable to fend off the attacks of the Portuguese. Others are of the opinion that Goans were already tapping and distilling toddy from the coconut trees to enjoy after a hard day's work (which, knowing Goans, I tend to believe more).

However, I recently learnt that the distillation process used for *feni* is similar to the one traditionally used for tequila. The tequila distillation process was brought to Mexico by Filipino workers who were taken to the country by the Spanish conquistadors, which makes me wonder if the Portuguese brought the methods with them from the Philippines. Given that the clergy transcended the Portugal-Spain border, this is quite probable.

Whatever the source, like the *choris*, it's Goan now. If you've never tasted *feni*, it's strong — stronger than tequila. The cashew version has a strong fruity smell and taste, which, let's be honest, requires an acclimatisation of the palate. The coconut version is just as alcoholic, but has a nuttier finish, which many find more refined and easier to acquire a taste for.

If *feni* is the drink that divides Goa, *urrack* is the one that unites it. This fruity, alcoholic juice-like drink is one that has Northerners and Southerners alike racing to the villages during March and April to get their annual quota. Everyone's a connoisseur, and everyone knows the best place to get it. Summer weekend afternoons are filled with conversations of comparisons, "*Arre*, this is just OK, you should try the one I got." It's the usual Goan male chauvinistic one-upmanship, riddled with Freudian phallic inadequacy and, as Shakespeare put it, "a great deal of nothing."

For those who are somewhat familiar with the making of alcohol, *urrack* is the product of the first distillation of fermented cashew juice, while the *cashew feni* is the product of the second distillation. *Feni* and *urrack* are still made traditionally in small batches with the cashews being stomped and crushed by foot (much like grapes) in makeshift wooden troughs in forest plantations. The juice (*niro*) is collected in jerry cans and transported to the fermentation stations, where it's stored in clay pots.

Clay Still used to distill urrack and feni

Once fermented, the juice is distilled over a wood fire, using what looks like the apparatus of a medieval alchemist, to get the first and lightest concentration of alcohol called *urrack*.

This is a delicious, light, and fruity drink whose potency tends to be underestimated — and dangerously so. Unlike *feni*, *urrack*, when mixed with carbonated lemonade, bitters, and garnished with a slit chilli (as is the customary cocktail through which the drink is consumed), tastes more like a refreshing pop or soda than an alcohol drink, inviting you to consume more. Also, unlike other alcohols, the inebriation is slow yet sudden. One moment, you're sitting in the shade of a coconut-thatched shack at the beach, enjoying the cool afternoon sea breeze; the next, you're staggering to the washroom with unhinged limbs that appear to have a mind of their own, unwilling to heed the commands of your brain, which of course–believes you could handle at least a couple more.

Chapter 10:
Monsoon Madness

The monsoons are a time of surplus water and scarcity of everything else. In the beginning, it's beautiful; the first drops of rain hit the dry red laterite soil, raising up small puffs of dust, and with it the wonderful, heady smell of wet mud, a smell that is to odours what manna is to food.

Petrichor is the word coined for it; a combination of the Greek words for stone, 'petra', and the liquid that was fabled to run through the veins of the Greek Gods, 'ichor'.

Within the first week of the rains, the outdoor colours change. They go from the dull brown-red hues of summer to every shade of green imaginable. The red soil, that is responsible for every Goan kid having to wash their tennis shoes (not to be confused with shoes used to play tennis, these were a part of the sports uniform for most schools, and were a weird rubber soled white canvas pair of shoes which was always laced up in the same parallel lace fashion) at least once a week, is no longer visible thanks to a dense cover of shrubbery and assorted weeds that sprung up as if by magic. It is the Goan equivalent of what spring would be for a cold country.

It's also the best season to move away from the beach and into the hills of the Western *Ghats* (mountain range). Streams, rivers, springs and waterfalls, which ran dry in the hot summer months, are suddenly full again.

And the higher up in the mountains you go, the clearer and crisper the water is. Downstream, however, the rivers – previously grey-blue – turn red-brown, filled with the aforementioned red laterite soil, which no longer bound by the roots of the great old trees that once held it in place, is free to elope with the rainwater, lending the marriage of earth and water its colouring.

Occasionally, you will find a remnant of the bondage of the earth by the forest in the form of the broken shackles of a tree floating in the river. It's this wonderful imagery that inspired me to come up with this dish of mine, which I call the "monsoon river".

Monsoon River

Monsoon River

Ingredients:

For the fish:

- 500 g boneless Fish, cut into 2 inch cubes
- ½ tsp Salt
- ¼ tsp Turmeric powder
- 1 Tbsp Oil for frying

For the gravy:

- 4 Tbsp Recheado Masala (or as required)
- 4 Tbsp water

For the pickled ginger and garlic:

- 1 clove of Garlic, cut into fine strips
- 1 inch Ginger, cut into fine strips
- ¼ cup Vinegar (Coconut or Apple Cider)
- 1 Tbsp Sugar
- ¼ cup Water

For the spinach log:

- 5 potatoes
- 1 Tbsp Butter
- 5 Spinach Leaves
- ½ tsp Salt

Method:

The fish:

1. Marinate the fish cubes with the salt and turmeric powder and set aside for at least an hour.

2. Place a pan over medium-high heat.

3. Add the oil and wait for it to heat.

4. Once the oil begins to shimmer, add in the fish skin side down and cook it for approximately 1 minute on each side.

5. Remove the fish from the pan and place it on a wire rack.

6. In the same pan, add the recheado masala and stir for a couple of minutes.

7. Once the masala begins to caramelize, add in the water and whisk to combine.

8. Bring the gravy to a boil and let it continue to boil down until it reaches a syrupy consistency.

9. Take off the heat and set aside until plating.

The spinach log:

1. Place the potatoes in a pan with water and boil until they are fork-tender.

2. Peel and mash the potatoes, adding salt and butter to taste.

3. Prepare an ice bath by placing ice and water into a large bowl.

4. Bring a pot of water to a boil over high heat.

5. Once the water is at a rolling boil, drop the spinach leaves in for about 2 minutes before removing them and placing them in the ice water.

6. Once the spinach leaves are cool, remove them from the ice water and let them dry on a paper towel, spreading the leaves out gently so as to retain their shape.

7. Take a dollop of mashed potato and spread it on each spinach leaf, covering the entire leaf.

8. Start at the end of the leaf with the stem and roll it towards the tip to form a log.

9. Keep about ¼ of the mashed potatoes for plating.

The ginger and garlic:

1. Place the ginger, garlic, water and vinegar into a pot and bring to a boil.

2. Add the sugar and stir to dissolve.

3. Allow it to boils for about 5 minutes, take it off the heat and let it cool.

Assembly:

1. Take a rectangular plate large enough to accommodate 5 cubes of fish in two parallel lines.

2. Place dollops of mashed potato in two parallel lines at the centre of the plate. There should be 3 dollops in one line and two in the other.

3. Over each dollop of mashed potato, place 1 piece of fish.

4. Pour the gravy onto the plate so that it surrounds the mashed potatoes and fish.

5. Place the spinach log between the pieces of fish.

6. Drain the ginger and garlic and use them to garnish the dish as you like.

7. Serve by itself or with rice.

By mid-monsoon, the romance is gone. The constant heavy rain causes a permeating dampness everywhere. Houses, clothes, cars and a little bit of your soul too, take on this heavy, gaseous, invisible fog, thick with the smell of mildew, decay and despair.

Everywhere you look, there is mould, and the odd day that the sun is shining is as welcome as the rains were when they first arrived. Worse, this was when we'd fall prey to stomach bugs. Fortunately, this is also when turmeric plants sprout foliage. If you believe old wives' tales and even older grandmother's remedies, turmeric leaves and palm sugar, along with a diet of mostly vegetarian food and a lot of pulses, are the best way to prevent or treat ailments. It was primarily during the monsoon that my grandmother would take up the preparation of *godshem* as an accompaniment for the afternoon tea. As mentioned before, *godshem* literally translates to "a little sweetness". It's usually a sweet made with a mixture of coconut, coconut milk, some type of beans, some cereal, and coconut jaggery. A nice warm bowl of this hearty, soulful concoction on a cold, damp day was just what the doctor (read "grandmother") ordered.

The sound of the wind blowing through the trees mingled with that of the ever-falling rain, modulating itself from a pitter-patter on the rooftops to a continuous maraca-like "shac-shac", felt like heaven.

Godshem

Ingredients (serves 4):

- 400 ml Coconut Cream
- ½ cup Matta or Goan Rice (or any short-grained variety, preferably brown)
- ½ cup Beans, soaked overnight (traditionally mung, black or red kidney beans, but you can use any other beans of your choosing)
- 2 cups of Water + more for washing
- 4 Tbsp - 1 cup Coconut Jaggery (as per your taste)
- ½ tsp Salt
- 1 Turmeric Leaf (optional)
- 2 pods of Green Cardamom (optional)

Method

1. Wash the rice in cold water until the water runs clear.
2. Put the rice and the drained, soaked beans into a stock pot with the water.
3. Add salt, bring to a boil, and then cover.

4. Let the pot simmer covered for about 15 minutes or until the water is all absorbed.

5. Now add in the turmeric leaf, the cardamom pods broken open, the coconut cream and the coconut jaggery.

6. Bring it to a boil over medium heat and cover.

7. Let it simmer for up to 5 minutes before taking it off the heat.

8. Serve hot or cold.

9. Refrigerate for up to one week.

My version of the dish combines multiple dishes that the term encapsulates, and is inspired by the monsoon phase of the Goan roads' cycle of death and resurrection. The roads, which were laid in the months prior to the drenching onslaught, get pockmarked and pitted with potholes that collect dirty water, making them look like a grey-brown rocky road.

Godshem - My Version

Godshem – My Version

Specific Equipment:

Ice-cream churner

Pressure cooker

Ingredients (serves 8-10):

For the base:

- 1 cup Rice (short-grained brown rice like Matta)
- 1 cup Mung Beans, soaked in water overnight
- 1 tsp Salt
- 2 cups of Water
- 4 Tbsp Coconut Jaggery

For the ice cream:

- 1 Turmeric Leaf (optional)
- 400 ml Coconut Cream
- ¼ cup Coconut Jaggery

For the sugar glaze:

- 1 cup of Water
- 1 cup Coconut Jaggery
- 3 Cardamom pods
- Chopped Nuts (optional)

Method:

The base:

1. Wash the rice under cold water until the water runs clear.

2. Drain the mung beans and put them into the pressure cooker with the rice, water, sugar and salt.

3. Pressure cook the rice for about 15 minutes.

4. Release the pressure and set it aside.

The ice-cream:

1. Put all the ingredients into a saucepan and bring to a boil.

2. Simmer for 3-5 minutes.

3. Take off the heat and let it cool to room temperature.

4. Remove and discard the turmeric leaf (if used).

5. Pour the mixture into the ice-cream churner and let it run until the ice-cream is formed.

6. Transfer the ice cream into a container and freeze.

The sugar glaze:

1. Combine all the ingredients in a saucepan and bring to a boil.

2. Let it boil until it reduces by $\frac{1}{3}^{rd}$ or gets thick enough to coat the back of a spoon.

3. Pour into a squeeze bottle.

Assembly:

1. Warm the rice and beans and place them on a plate to form the base of the road.

2. Sprinkle chopped nuts onto the "road".

3. Place a scoop of the ice cream on one end and drizzle the sugar glaze over the entire road.

The scarcity of the monsoons is not limited to sunlight. It's pretty much everything. There's no fish, because boats won't go out to sea, discouraged either by the high winds and large swells or the month-long fishing ban imposed to ensure fish propagate enough to let their future generations fall prey to ours, in a fast, thinning cycle of "sustainable" carnivorous consumption. There are limited vegetables because every available field is engaged in the cultivation of rice, and most everything else is out of season.

It's a time when traditionally, Goans relied on pickles, preserves and cures to quench their thirst for proteins. Out come the *paras* (pickled fish), the *miscuts* and the *chempnis* that were so painstakingly made during the summer. There are, of course, vegetarian options for protein as well, like *dals* (lentils), beans and other pulses. But it is the time of year when the smell of *haaren* (charred salted fish) and pungent coconut vinegar fills the air during lunch time. The time when the vegetables available to eat are either from your garden or pickled. Of course, this was the Goa of yore, the one where you ate what grew or was caught in your village or, at most, the neighbouring villages. Today, thanks to larger carbon footprints, better transportation and the desire to abandon the less dignified and lower-paying professions in favour of "office jobs", everything is available throughout the year. With this almost superfluous abundance, we lose traditions and recipes but gain writers, the likes of myself, who live in their heads, comforted by the recipes of grandmothers, and nostalgia of the "good old days", which may not have been good, or for that matter, old.

Dal Tadka

Dal Tadka with rice & pickle

Specific Equipment:

Pressure cooker

Ingredients (serves 4-5):

- 1 cup split Red Lentils, soaked for 1 hour to overnight
- 2 cloves of Garlic
- 1 tsp Salt
- 2 cups of Water
- 2 Tbsp neutral Oil
- 1 Tbsp Red Mustard Seeds
- 1 cup chopped Red Onion
- 2 sprigs of Curry Leaves (16-20 leaves)
- 1 tsp Cumin
- ¼ tsp Fenugreek Seeds
- 2 dried Red Chillies (or curd chillies)
- 2 Tbsp Coriander Leaves, chopped fine

Method:

1. Drain the red lentils.
2. Add the lentils, garlic, salt and water to the pressure cooker.
3. Pressure cook the lentils for 1 hour and then let the pressure release naturally.
4. Open the pressure cooker and, using a whisk, mash the lentils and garlic together to form a thick gravy. You can adjust the consistency by adding water.

5. Place the pressure cooker on medium-low heat (without the lid) and bring to a simmer.

6. Pour the oil into a pan and place it over a medium-high heat.

7. Once the oil is hot, add in the mustard seeds. They should begin to splutter.

8. Once the popping slows to about 1 second between pops, add in the cumin, fenugreek, curry leaves and chillies.

9. Sauté the mixture for about a minute or two.

10. Add in the onions and sauté until the onions are translucent.

11. Pour the contents of the pan into the pressure cooker and stir to combine.

12. Take the mixture off the heat and add the coriander leaves.

13. Serve over rice with pickles on the side.

The monsoons do bring out a different set of animals to satiate the carnivores in us. Fields flood with water, as is required for rice cultivation. These floods awaken a network of canals, streams, and mini-rivers along well-eroded courses which, during summer, could very well be mistaken for gorges or rift valleys. These streams fill quickly with freshwater catfish like *tigur* and *sangot*. The fields themselves fill with snails called *congem*, which are promptly collected to be cooked into either a chilli-fry or an *xacuti*-style curry. The other favourite during the monsoon is what is now (illegally) sold in restaurants as "jumping chicken". For the uninitiated, this is code for frog, to be specific, the Indian bullfrog, which has been hunted to near extinction in the state.

Frog hunting was an art with Goans. They'd go out at night and follow the croaks to locate the jumpers. It is not as easy as it sounds. You wade through thigh-deep muck, listening to a cacophony of hundreds of different animals, including other frogs, for a particular croak, and then try and determine where the croak came from. You'd then move in the direction of the croak in the darkness, flash a light into the eyes of the amphibian to shock it into temporary paralysis, pick it up and put it into your sack.

Frog legs were a sought-after delicacy in Goa. Thankfully, with the growing awareness of the plight of the endangered frogs and the reluctance of the younger generation to eat "icky" things, consumption has reduced.

Purmentachem Fest

Disclaimer: In this part, I am referring to the old church of the 1800s and early 1900s. None of what follows should be used in a present-day context.

Catholicism is a hardy religion, and my theory is that it's hardy because of its employment of enforcement and absorption. The early Catholics were smart; they used an unbeatable combination of coercion and guilt, followed by reward, to grow the religion. The way in which it was done was almost artful. They started with coercion through the inquisition: "Accept our

Lord and Saviour, or suffer." Then they laid on the guilt: "You are a good Catholic; the lord wants you to make others accept Him as you have." And finally, they involved absorption: "You celebrate the winter solstice? What a coincidence, Jesus was born on the 25th of December, you can celebrate that instead."

A great example of absorption in Goa is the *Purmentachem Fest* (Feast of Pentecost). This feast is a celebration of Pentecost and falls just before the commencement of the monsoon, so the churches of both major cities in North and South Goa (i.e., Panaji and Margao) celebrate it. My guess is that this festival occurred in some form even before the arrival of the Portuguese, and during their rule, they replaced the traditional festival, whatever it was, with *Purmentachem fest*.

In Margao, the Old Market area (very innovatively named), located in the vicinity of the Holy Spirit Church, turned into a sort of fairgrounds with games, rides, and vendors selling their wares. This was not unlike any other feast in Goa. However, this particular feast had a special set of vendors who would not be found at most other feasts. These were what I call the "provision vendors." As this feast occurs just before the monsoons, it presented the perfect opportunity to stock up on pickles and sun-dried provisions that were staples during the monsoon.

The "provision vendors" would sell sun-dried fish, pickles, tamarind, chillies, dried mangoes, coconut vinegar and other such non-perishables. The feast was meant for the city folk who didn't have the time, patience, or will to do the drying and pickling themselves. It also presented an opportunity for the village folk to sell off their surplus and make some money for the monsoon.

While the feast was a marketplace for all provisions, a special emphasis must be laid on the sale of dry fish. This one-time necessity is today a delicacy. Even in the early 1990s, dry fish was a necessity due to the lack of fish during this season, save for the odd river fish caught by the farmer while ploughing his fields.

Dry Shrimp/Prawns and Okra Solantulem

This was a very popular monsoon dish in my household when I was a kid. It's a sour, watery curry eaten with rice. It's light and flavourful, and made with only a few ingredients – by Goan standards. This dish was also made when someone was sick and needed something light, but flavourful, to eat.

Ingredients (serves 6-7):

- 300 g Okra, cut into 1 inch rounds
- 200 g large Dried Shrimp/Prawns
- 2 Shallots (or 1 onion), sliced into half moons
- 6 cloves of Garlic
- 1 inch Ginger
- 1 tsp Cumin
- 1 tsp Black Peppercorns
- ¼ tsp Turmeric powder

- 1 inch Cinnamon stick

- 4 whole Cloves

- ¾ cup Water or as needed

- 1 Tbsp Tamarind, soaked in warm water for about an hour

- 3-4 Kokum pieces

- 2 Green Chillies (optional)

- Salt as needed

Method:

1. In a heavy-bottomed pan, toast the dry shrimp/prawns until fragrant and slightly charred (do not burn them, they just need to get some colour).

2. Remove the shrimp/prawns from the pan and set aside.

3. In the same pan, add the water, onions, garlic, ginger, chillies and spices, and bring to a boil.

4. Add the tamarind water, kokum, and okra and cover the pan.

5. Let it simmer for about 3 minutes.

6. Add in the dry shrimp/prawns and let it simmer for 2 more minutes.

7. Taste and adjust the seasoning with salt and tamarind water.

8. Serve as a soup or over rice.

Note:

- You can add a tsp of sugar to round off the flavour.

Dry Fish Salad

Ingredients:

- 200 g Dried Fish (The most commonly used are mackerel, Bombay duck or stingray, but you can use anchovies, shrimp/prawns or even dry squid.)
- 1 large Onion, diced
- 1 Tomato, diced
- 1-2 Green Chillies, minced
- Coriander Leaves, minced
- 1 Tbsp Vinegar (Coconut or Apple Cider)
- 1 Tbsp Coconut Oil

Method:

1. Debone the fish, if using mackerel. If using any other fish, skip this step.
2. Pour the oil into a pan and place it over medium heat.
3. Toast the fish until it starts to char (do not burn it, it just needs to get some colour).
4. Set the charred fish aside to cool.
5. Combine the rest of the ingredients in a bowl.

6. Once cool, shred the fish into bite-sized pieces and add to the salad.

Note:

- This is an excellent side dish and a great accompaniment for a fish curry over rice.

- Adding toasted peanuts to the salad, while not traditional, adds another dimension.

Kismoor

Ingredients:

- 1 cup Shredded Coconut

- 1 cup Dried Shrimp/Prawns

- 1 large Onion, diced

- 1 tsp Kashmiri Chilli powder

- ¼ tsp Turmeric powder

- 1 sprig of Curry Leaves (8-10 leaves)

- 1 tsp Tamarind, soaked in 2 Tbsp warm water for about an hour

- 2-3 Kokum pieces

- 2 Green Chillies (optional)

Method:

1. In a heavy-bottomed pan, toast the dry shrimp/prawns until fragrant and slightly charred (do not burn them, they just need to get some colour).

2. Remove the shrimp/prawns from the pan and set aside.

3. Pour the oil into the same pan.

4. Add the onions and sauté until translucent.

5. Add in the turmeric, chilli, curry leaves, and coconut.

6. Sauté the mixture on medium heat until the coconut releases oil.

7. Wring out all the juices of the tamarind into the water it was soaking in. Discard the wrung tamarind and pour the tamarind water into the pan.

8. Add in the kokum and mix well.

9. Add the shrimp/prawns and sauté for a few more minutes.

10. Take the pan off the heat.

11. Serve with rice and curry.

PART 4:

THE NORTH-SOUTH DIVIDE

Chapter 11:
Lost in Translation:
Dialects and Languages

If you've been reading in sequence, you'll notice that there's a lot of talk of how Northerners (North Goans) or Southerners (South Goans) "do it differently." I feel the need to shed some light on the great north-south divide.

There is a tendency for people to harp on differences rather than come together on commonalities - something observed in older civilisations that are steeped in traditions and culture. I believe it has to do with there being only one "right way" of doing things. You won't see much of this in newer colonies like North America or Australia. But as a community ages, much like people, it gets set in its ways, and that leads to the "we do it that way" attitude.

In India, it's everywhere. It's a kind of hyper-local, hyper-religious, hyper-cultural establishment and enforcement of one's values, traditions, and even recipes. To an extent, it's an intolerance of sorts that manifests in different ways.

In Goa, you see it in the mildly passive-aggressive ribbing between friends' on the basis of the words they use (or don't use), their pronunciation, their dialect, along with stereotyping - "*Xastikars* (people from the Taluka of Salcette) are miserly",

166

"*Moirekars* (people from Moira) are eccentric (read as: stupid and crazy)," etc.

Today, the distinctions are more diluted, perhaps due to intermingling of the villages through marriage, or maybe the arrival of "outsiders" (non-Goans), who have become the new targets. Or it could be a result of the dwindling population of what I like to call "aristocratically heritaged Goans" – Goans who can trace their ancestry back at least ten generations. Whatever the reason, it's a welcome step in the direction of genuine unity in diversity. A celebration of our differences with "You say *Poiee*, I say *Bhakri*, but we are all *Paos*." For those who don't understand Konkani, a particular bread is called *poiee* by North Goans and *bhakri* by South Goans. And while *pao* is another type of bread, the term is also a slur for a country bumpkin.

Konkani is one of the most unique languages. It was initially thought to be a dialect of Marathi (another Indian language), but it has too many intricacies and dialects of its own to be just a dialect. Konkani is spoken along the entire Konkan coast, which spreads right from Mumbai (Vassai) in the north, to Mangaluru in the South, and even includes a small part of Northern Kerala. Even though the dialect changes every three kilometers, for the most part, we all understand each other and can even identify which area one hails from based on the dialect they speak.

What's really unique is that along this entire coast, even the script in which the language is written changes. In the states of Maharashtra and Goa, the language is largely written in the

Devanagari script, which is the same script in which Hindi and Marathi are written (with a few different alphabets). In Goa, Hindus write Konkani in the Devanagari script, but Catholics use the Roman script, which was taught to us by the clergy. All Catholic religious texts that were translated into Konkani are in the Roman script. Travel further south to Karnataka, and Konkani is written in the Kannada script, which is a Dravidian script. And even further south, in Kerala, Konkani is written in the Malayalam script. And that's why even though we can communicate with each other through speech, we cannot write to each other.

Within the state of Goa itself, Konkani has two different scripts and at least three major dialects. Goa has 12 *talukas* (districts), and in each, you'll find a few words that differ from the others. However, broadly, two major Catholic dialects emerge: North Goan Konkani (also known as "Bardez Konkani", after the *taluka* with the same name) and South Goan Konkani (also known as "*xashti* Konkani", after the *taluka* of Salcette). And then there's the Hindu dialect, which has its own nuances.

My wife and I are from different parts of Goa; I'm from the South, and she's from the North. For the most part, we can understand each other's Konkani, but occasionally we come across words that we've not heard before.

Map of Goa showing North Goa and South Goa

The South Goan dialect has more of a drawl and a sing-song rhythm with a lot of emphasis on the 'sh' sounds. Most vowels at the end of a word are dropped. Whereas the North Goan dialect removes the 'sh' sound if it occurs in the middle of a word, and every vowel is properly pronounced, but *a's* in this dialect gives a more rounded 'O' sound.

As an example, if I were to say "How are you?" in North Goan Konkani, it would be:

Koho aha re tu?

While in the South Goan dialect it would be:

Kesh aha re tu?

And in the Hindu dialect, it would be:

Koso assa re tum?

Here's a list of a few words that are used differently in North and South Goan dialects.

English	North Goan Dialect	South Goan Dialect
Mussels	Xinanio	Zob
Whole wheat flat bread	Poiee	Bhakri
Unleavened flatbread (aka chapati)	Bhakri	Choupati
Whole wheat bread roll	Unde	Paunce
Forward	Fudem	Mukaar

Chapter 12:
United we Eat,
Divided we Cook

The North-South divide is especially obvious when it comes to food. The preparations are very different. In the South (where I'm from), we add a little sweetness to everything, whereas in the North, it is spicier and more sour. There are also some dishes that the other side has never heard about.

Some of these dishes are:

- **Samarachi Kodi,** a North Goan curry made with dry shrimp/prawns and bilimbis served during the *bui jevan* ceremony of the Goan wedding (more details in the wedding section later).

- **Aaran,** a South Goan steamed curry paste with small bait fish or kingfish.

- **Balchao,** a dish that is prepared very different in North and South Goa. In the South, it is a pickle made of dried shrimp/prawns fry (baby shrimp/prawns called *galmo* in Konkani). But in the North, it is a dish made with fresh shrimp/prawns in a base made of dry shrimp/prawns and garlic paste.

- **Aad Maas** (literal translation: bony meat), once again a dish that's very different in North and South Goa. In the

South, it's a light watery gravy with pork bones, and flavoured with a basic *jeerem-meerem* masala and a lot of *binda sol* or tamarind. In the North, it's a spicy, thick curry.

- *Crab Xec Xec* is also different in the North and South. In the North, it takes on more of a dry xacuti-like dish, but in the South, it's a sweet-spicy dish with tomato, chilli, garlic, ginger, onion, a hint of *garam masala*, and coconut.

Samarachi Kodi

Specific Equipment:

Mixer grinder or food processor

Ingredients (serves 4-6):

For the spice blend:

- 1½ Tbsp Coriander seeds
- 1½ Tbsp Fennel seeds
- 1 tsp Cumin seeds
- 1 tsp Black Peppercorns
- 6 Kashmiri Red Chillies
- 1 Tbsp White Peas (or Chickpeas)
- ¼ tsp Fenugreek seeds
- ¼ tsp Mustard seeds
- 1 pod Cardamom

- ½ inch Cinnamon stick

- 1 petal of Mace

- 1 petal of Star Anise

- 5 whole Cloves

- ¼ tsp Turmeric powder

- ¼ tsp Nutmeg powder

For the base:

- 1 Onion, diced fine

- 2 cups Coconut Cream

- 1 Tbsp Oil

- 2 sprigs Curry Leaves

- 1 green Mango seed or 2 dry Green Mango slices or 1 tsp *Aamchur* (dried mango) powder

- ½ cup Dried Shrimp/Prawns

Method:

1. Place a skillet or frying pan over medium-low heat.

2. Dry roast each of the spice blend ingredients separately in the pan until they are fragrant, then set them aside to cool. Do not roast the ingredients all together as they cook at different rates and may burn.

3. Once all the spice blend ingredients are roasted and cooled, place them in a grinder/food processor and grind them to a fine powder.

4. In a sauce pot, heat oil over a medium heat.

5. Add the onions and sauté until they start to brown.

6. Add the curry leaves and the dried shrimp/prawns, and sauté for about 2 minutes.

7. Add the spice blend and stir well.

8. Pour in the coconut cream and stir to incorporate.

9. Add the mango/*aamchur* and bring the curry to a boil.

10. Once it boils, lower the heat to low and allow the curry to simmer for 10 minutes.

11. Serve with plain steamed rice.

South Goan Beef Stew

Ingredients (serves 4-6):

- 500 g Beef, cubed

- 1 Tbsp Garlic paste

- ½ Tbsp Ginger paste

- 1 tsp Cumin powder

- 1 tsp Ground Black Pepper

- ¼ tsp Turmeric powder

- 4 whole Cloves

- 2 inch Cinnamon stick

- 2 pods Cardamom

- 1 petal of Star Anise
- 1 Onion, diced fine
- 1 large Carrot, diced
- 2 large Potatoes, diced
- 1-2 tsp Salt (as per taste)
- 1 Tbsp Oil
- 1 cup Dry Elbow Macaroni or other pasta (penne/spirali, farfalle, etc) cooked as per package instructions
- ¼ cup Heavy Cream

Method:

1. Mix the ginger paste, garlic paste, cumin, turmeric, pepper, and salt together and apply it to the meat. Mix well to ensure it's well coated and set aside for at least an hour or overnight in the fridge.
2. Place a large pot over medium heat and pour in the oil.
3. Add in the onions, carrots, and whole spices and sauté.
4. Once the onions start to caramelize, add in the potatoes.
5. Season with a little salt.
6. Add in the cubes of meat and stir so they get seared on all sides.
7. Add in water to cover the meat (1-2 cups) and cover the pot while it comes to a boil.
8. After about 10 minutes, stir in the cooked pasta and cream

9. Let the dish come to a boil again, and then turn off the heat.

10. Serve with *pulao* or *pao*.

South Goan Prawn Balchao

Traditionally, in South Goa, this is a pickle that was eaten during the monsoons when fish was scarce. This pickle requires an ingredient only available in South Goa: the *galmo bhakri*. The *galmo bhakri* is a cake of dry shrimp/prawns, made by forming shrimp/prawn fry (baby shrimp/prawns) into a patty and then sun-drying the patty. I believe that this dish was introduced to Goa by travellers (most likely the Portuguese) from Burma, where they make a similar dish out of dry shrimp/prawns and onions called 'Balachung'. But whatever the origin, it's delicious. It's unlikely that you will find *galmo bhakri* outside of Goa. The alternative is dry shrimp/prawns, but try and find the smallest possible dry shrimp/prawns for this recipe. The traditional Goan recipe also calls for coconut *feni*, the local alcohol made from the sap of the coconut tree. I find that vodka or tequila is a good substitute.

Ingredients (1 ½ kg):

- 1 kg Tiny Dried Shrimp/Prawns
- 2 Tbsp Garlic paste
- ¼ cup Coconut Vinegar
- 2 tsp Ground Black Pepper
- 2 Tbsp Kashmiri Chilli powder

- ¼ cup Coconut *Feni* (use Tequila/Vodka, or if you prefer alcohol free, use more Vinegar)
- ½ tsp Turmeric powder
- 1 Tbsp Salt
- 2 Tbsp Sugar
- 2 cups Oil

Method:

1. Soak the dry shrimp/prawns in the vinegar for an hour until they rehydrate.

2. Mix all the spice powders together with the salt.

3. Heat oil in a pan until it is at deep frying temperature (350°F) and pour it carefully over the spice mix. Do this in a heat-proof container or stock pot, as the oil will agitate.

4. Add in the shrimp/prawns soaked in vinegar along with the alcohol (*feni*/tequila/vodka) while the oil is still hot but not sizzling.

5. Store this in a clean, sterilized jar and let it mature for 2 weeks before eating.

6. Eat it as a condiment with rice, *pez*, or in a sandwich.

North Goan Prawn Balchao

In North Goa, prawn *balchao* is a dish, as opposed to a condiment. The North Goan prawn *balchao* uses the South Goan prawn *balchao* as a base and adds some *recheado* masala and fresh shrimp/prawns to it. It's something that confused me when I first visited a restaurant and saw the dish on a menu. I wrote it off as an innovation by the restaurant. Later, when I met my wife, I learnt that this was just the way prawn *balchao* was served in the North.

Ingredients (serves 8-10):

- 1 kg Fresh Shrimp/Prawns, deveined and shelled
- ½ tsp Turmeric powder
- 1-2 tsp Salt
- 2 Tbsp South Goan *Balchao*
- 4 Tbsp *Recheado* Masala
- 2 Onions, diced fine
- 1 Tbsp Oil

Method:

1. Marinate the shrimp/prawns with the turmeric powder and salt for about ½ an hour.
2. Pour the oil into a pan placed over medium heat.
3. Fry the shrimp/prawns until they are just cooked through and set them aside.
4. In the same pan, add more oil, if required, and add the onions.
5. Sauté the onions until they begin to brown.

6. Add in the *recheado* masala and cook, stirring constantly until the oil begins to separate.

7. Add the South Goan *balchao* and reduce the heat to low.

8. Add the shrimp/prawns and stir to coat evenly with the masala.

9. Taste and adjust the seasoning for salt and sugar.

10. Once the shrimp/prawns are warmed through, turn off the heat and serve over steamed rice or with *pao*.

Aaran

Specific Equipment:

Mixer grinder or food processor

Ingredients (serves 4-6):

- 500 g Small Bait Fish or Kingfish Steaks (also works well with sole, ray, shark, or even halibut)
- 6-8 dry Kashmiri Red Chillies
- 6 cloves of Garlic
- 2 inches Ginger, peeled
- 2 whole Cloves
- 1 inch Cinnamon stick
- 1 tsp Pepper
- 1 tsp Cumin
- ¼ cup Vinegar

- 1-2 tsp Sugar
- 1 + ½ tsp salt
- ¼ tsp Turmeric powder
- 1 tsp Tamarind
- 1 Large Onion, diced fine

Method:

1. Place the ginger, garlic, chillies, cumin, pepper, cinnamon, tamarind, cloves, vinegar, sugar, and 1 tsp salt in the grinder/food processor and grind to a fine paste.

2. Sprinkle ½ tsp salt and the turmeric evenly onto the fish.

3. Combine the onions with the spice paste.

4. If using bait fish, you can combine the bait fish into the mixture and mix to coat. If using other fish, apply the mixture to the fish and layer the fish in a deep crock-pot.

5. Place the pot on low heat and cover.

6. Let the fish steam in the paste for about 15-20 minutes or until the fish is cooked through.

Aad Maas

This dish literally translates to "meat on bone". This is a basic peasant recipe made with the cheaper cuts of pork that are primarily bone. In the South, it is a thin gravy, almost like a soup, which is served over rice. It's sour from the tamarind or kokum, and the pork lends the dish a little sweetness. It's mildly spiced with pepper, cumin, and green chilli.

In the North, *aad maas* is thicker and spicier, made with more dried chillies and soured with vinegar instead of tamarind.

The South Goan version is basically a dish called *solantulem* but made with pork bones instead of other, fleshier cuts. This is also South Goa's go-to recipe for pork trotters or dried shrimp/prawns during the monsoons. The word *solantulem* literally translates to "cooked with dried slices". *Solam* is Konkani for "bits or slices of sour fruit sun-dried to preserve them". The two most used in Goan cuisine are *aam sol* (dried green mango slices) and *binda sol* (dried *kokum* or Indian mangosteen skins).

I don't know much about the North Goan versions because those were something we ate only at restaurants or when we visited friends from North Goa, and with the divide being as it is, we wouldn't admit that their version was as good as ours.

South Goan Aad Maas

Ingredients (serves 4-6):

- 500 g Pork Bones (use knuckles, riblets or even trotters)
- 4 large Onions, sliced
- 6-8 cloves of Garlic
- 1 inch Ginger, sliced
- 1 inch Cinnamon stick
- 3 whole Cloves
- 1 tsp Black Peppercorns
- 2 tsp Salt
- ¼ tsp Turmeric powder
- ½ tsp Cumin
- 2-4 Thai Green Chillies, slit
- 1 tsp of Tamarind, soaked in ½ cup warm water or 12 slices of Kokum pieces
- 1 tsp Sugar (optional)

Method:

1. Marinate the pork in salt and turmeric powder. Mix well to coat and set aside in the fridge for at least one hour.

2. Put the pork and all the other ingredients except the tamarind/kokum into a stock pot over low heat, and cover. The heat should be as low as possible.

3. In about 15 minutes, uncover the pot and add the tamarind pulp through a strainer (to discard the seeds and fibrous content of the tamarind). If you're using *kokum*, add that instead of the tamarind.

4. Top the pork with water as needed (2 cups is recommended, but you can adjust as per your preference).

5. Cover and let it simmer for about 2 hours, stirring occasionally and adding water as needed.

6. Add the sugar, if using.

7. Serve over plain steamed rice.

North Goan Aad Maas

Specific Equipment:

Mixer grinder or food processor

Ingredients (serves 4-6):

- 500 g Pork Bones (use knuckles, riblets or even trotters)
- 4 Large Onions, sliced
- 1 tsp Tamarind, soaked in ½ cup warm water

For the masala:

- 6-8 cloves of Garlic
- 1 inch Ginger, sliced
- 1 inch Cinnamon stick
- 3 whole Cloves
- 1 tsp Black Peppercorns
- 2 tsp Salt
- ¼ tsp Turmeric powder
- ½ tsp Cumin
- ¼ cup Coconut Vinegar
- 8 Kashmiri Red Chillies
- 1 tsp Sugar (optional)

Method:

1. Place all the masala ingredients in the grinder/food processor and grind them into a smooth paste.

2. Pour the paste over the pork and let it marinate for at least an hour and up to overnight, in the fridge.

3. In a stock pot, arrange the sliced onions to cover the bottom.

4. Place the marinated pork with all of the marinade over the onions.

5. Place the pot on low heat and cover for about 15 minutes.

6. Add the tamarind pulp through a strainer (to discard the seeds and fibrous content of the tamarind).

7. Top the pork with water as needed (2 cups is recommended, but you can adjust as per your preference).

8. Cover and let it simmer covered for about 2 hours, stirring occasionally and adding water as needed.

9. Add the sugar, if using.

10. Serve over plain steamed rice.

PART 5:

SPECIAL

OCCASIONS

Chapter 13:
Blessed be the Food

A part of living in a middle-class Catholic family was reciting the rosary together. This was usually flagged off by the church's Angelus bell, which rang punctually at 7 p.m. every day. A family affair steeped in tradition, it was adopted from the Portuguese by our ancestors, for whom the religion into which they were born held little meaning when compared to the land, possessions, dignity, and life they would be relieved of had they not accepted the Lord and Saviour (Read as: Inquisitioned).

A little-known fact about Goan history is that we suffered a long inquisition from 1560 right up to 1820, when it was abolished. During this time, the natives, who consisted of Jews, Muslims, Hindus, and Buddhists, mixed in with a few other religions of the time, were tortured, imprisoned, and even burnt at the stake for practising their respective faiths. The fervour with which the Goan Catholics adhere to the timetable set forth by the church bells is just generational trauma.

It wasn't so much about belief as it was about survival. Of course, the latest descendants of these converted ancestors either take a lax view towards religion or fervently follow the traditions and rituals of the Catholic faith in the hope of salvation, which, as per the Saviour, has already been granted.

The rosary was presided over by the patriarch of the household. Goan society, like most of India, was quite patriarchal. However, I've been told, on many occasions, my great-grandmother would take charge and even defy my great-grandfather. It was done very subtly, making sure that his pride and ego were not publicly bruised. In many ways, it was an art, and my great-grandmother executed it with panache.

In one such incident, my great-grandfather had knocked back one *feni* too many before the rosary, and I'm told, the rosary went on for more than the church mandated five decades. Even after the regular half-hour allotted for prayers was up, my great-grandfather showed no signs of stopping or even slowing down. The holy activity was beginning to eat into bath time, which would delay dinner and other pre-bed activities. Back in those days, you didn't question the patriarch. No one did, not even his adult married children who had their own brood.

So after what seemed like the 100th decade of the rosary (everyone gave up counting), my great-grandmother burst into a hymn, much like they do at the Oscars once you've exceeded your time limit for the speech. At the end of the hymn, she simply went up to the altar, blew out the candles, and told the kids to go get the blessings of the elders. As per my grandmother, everyone was shocked into silence—but they obeyed. And great-grandfather, sensing something amiss, timidly gave his blessings, his only comment being, "It's nice that we started singing hymns after the rosary." Since that day, every rosary in the house ended with a hymn, which, considering that my family isn't gifted with vocal talents, is less than ideal.

On Sundays and special occasions, the rosary was followed by the *ladainha* (litany): a responsorial recitation of a list of saints, relics, and different apparitions of the Virgin Mary or Queen Mary, asking them to either graciously hear us or pray for us. Once again, if you were middle, upper-middle, or upper class, this was sung in Latin. Yes, you read that right — Latin.

As a kid, all you knew was that you were to respond with "*Ora Pronobis*" in a nice, long sing-song manner so that it sounded a bit like Aww-ra-Pro-nawww-bis. If you're a Goan Catholic, you probably sang it in your head, right? If not, we'll ask your Goan Catholic friend to sing it for you.

The *ladainha* was also recited during the Novenas, the nine days leading up to feasts, similar to the 'navratri' before Dussehra in the Hindu calendar.

On a side note, there are a lot of similarities in the practices or rituals of almost all religions in the world, which should make it easier for us to appreciate each other's faiths. But alas, we're happy counting conversions and *ghar wapsi* (re-conversions), rather than truly seeking God.

Getting back on track, those *ladainhas* were a great source of joy for us as kids. No, we didn't care about the prayers or the spirituality of it. It was just that it was conducted after dark, a time when we weren't usually allowed outdoors, it was followed by snacks, and if you were lucky, Rasna (a do-it-yourself chemistry set consisting of powders, concentrated

190

syrups, and God knows what else, which had to be combined, boiled and diluted, before being chilled and served). Rasna was sugary, sweet and probably full of artificial flavours and colours. But we, as kids, loved it and relished every last drop of it, all the while reciting, "I love you, Rasna" – the product's slogan.

Ladainha snacks ranged from biscuits and samosas to the rare but beloved snack platter (which I dare say is more indicative of a Goan Catholic celebration than anything else), consisting of a beef croquette, fish paté on fried bread, a Russian salad canapé, and a triangle of chutney sandwich. Sometimes, if shrimp/prawns were cheap, you'd get a *rissois* instead of the fish paté on toast.

Goan Snack Platter (*clockwise from bottom-left*: Croquettes, Rissois and Chutney Sandwich)

Fish on Toast

Ingredients (makes 40 mini toasts):

- 250 g Canned Sardines
- 4 Tbsp Butter
- 10 slices of White Bread
- 5 Tbsp Oil

Method:

1. Drain the oil/water from the sardines and place them in a bowl.

2. Add the butter and, using a fork, smash together to make a paste as smooth as possible.

3. Cut off the crust of the slices of bread, and then cut each slice into quarters.

4. Place a pan with the oil over high heat and wait until the oil begins to shimmer.

5. Place as many pieces of bread that fit flat into the hot pan.

6. Fry the bread until it's golden brown on both sides.

7. Remove the bread from the pan and let it cool on a wire rack.

8. Spread the sardine paste on the bread, and it's ready to serve.

9. You can garnish it with some finely diced raw onion and tomato if you like.

Chutney Sandwich

The quintessential Goan snack that's stood the test of time. When I was a child, my mom would always have a batch of green coconut chutney in the fridge, and whenever I was hungry, I'd just spread some on white bread with butter and have an instant, satisfying snack.

Specific Equipment:

Mixer-grinder or food processor

Ingredients:

For the spread:

- 1 cup fresh shredded Coconut
- 1 cup Coriander Leaves
- 2 Green Chillies
- 4-6 cloves of Garlic
- 1 inch Ginger
- 1 tsp Salt
- 1 tsp Tamarind
- 1 tsp ground Black Pepper
- 1 tsp Cumin
- 3 whole Cloves

- 1 inch Cinnamon stick

- 1 Tbsp Sugar

- ½ cup Water (or as needed)

For the sandwich (makes two triangle sandwiches):

- 2 slices of White Bread

- Butter

Method:

Green coconut chutney:

1. Place all the ingredients, except water, in the grinder/food processor.

2. Pulse until it starts to break down.

3. Turn on the grinder and add 1 Tbsp of water at a time until the contents form a smooth, thick paste with the consistency of cream cheese.

4. Refrigerate for up to 2 weeks.

The sandwich:

1. Butter one side of one slice of bread.

2. Spread the chutney on one side of the other slice of bread.

3. Close the sandwich and cut it in half diagonally.

Notes:

- This is a simple chutney sandwich and is usually served along with other snacks like croquettes and/or *rissois*. One way we enjoyed eating it was to insert a croquette into the sandwich and eat it together.

- If you add some light Swiss cheese, like an Emmental, or even a slice of plain old processed cheese, it adds a nice dimension.

Chapter 14:
Celebrations on the Streets

India, in general, is known for its celebrations on the streets. Fireworks during 'Diwali', 'Ganesh Visarjans' (where statues of Lord Ganesh are immersed into water bodies at the end of their 5, 7, 11 or 21-day worship), parades during 'Holi', etc.

Goa is no different when it comes to street celebrations. To quote Bon Jovi, "It's all the same, only the names will change," and now, to paraphrase him, every day it seems we're celebrating away.

The list of festivals celebrated in this state is long. There are festivals and *pujas* for things you'd never imagine possible. Some are very sombre and macabre, even conducted under strict no-filming and photography rules, while others are joyous and inclusive, inviting all to participate.

Despite the small size of the state, the regions are diverse, with each village having its own unique cultural celebrations. One that absolutely deserves more than a mention is the Zambaulim *Shigmo*, which is celebrated much like 'Holi' is in the rest of India, with 'gulal' (coloured powder traditionally made from turmeric treated with slacked lime to give it a red hue).

To say that this is a Spring festival would be to strip it of its meaning. This festival involves multiple legends and gods, the most popular one being a celebration of Lord Krishna (known as Lord Damodar in Goa) and Radha. There is also a procession of Lord Malikarjun (an incarnation of Lord Shiva).

Zambaulim *Shigmo* is very important to the Goan Hindu community, especially in South Goa, particularly, Margao. Back when Goa was under the Portuguese rule and the Inquisition, a lot of temples in the state were destroyed, and churches were built in their place. One of these was the Shri Damodar Temple of Margao (then known as Mathagram or "place of monasteries"). But the resilient and defiant community managed to smuggle out the statues (the word "idol" has been tarnished by Western use) of the deities and whisked them away to Zambaulim in the far south east, an area which, though under Portuguese rule, was not frequented by them. Here, they were housed in a new temple complex.

I personally behold this temple as a monument of sacrifice, perseverance, and defiance against oppressive rule.

The inhabitants of Goa who weren't able to defy or otherwise escape their tormentors had no choice but to accept their new Lord and Saviour. As part of their indoctrination, they had to give up everything about their culture and beliefs and exchange them for new church-sanctioned ones. They could no longer participate in celebrations of other religious festivals for fear of being inquisitioned, their land taken away, and their kin tortured and killed by the government while the church prayed for their immortal souls.

My Grandparents rarely spoke of it. It was too traumatic for them, I suspect. But every once in a while, a snippet of a story would leak out about how someone's whole family was killed because they had a hint of colour on them after *Shigmo* celebrations. As kids, we were curious and wanted to know more, but our questions were hushed by our parents, who thought it better to hide the horrors than confront their own conflict of faith. This has unfortunately resulted in a complete erasure of centuries of oppression by the colonists, with most Catholics of my generation unbelieving of these facts, writing them off as "fake news" spread by the Hindu right wing to create a divide.

But coming back to the celebrations, Catholics have a bunch of celebrations of their own: Feasts. Feasts are generally in celebration of one of the numerous saints of the Catholic religion. They are celebrated by all churches around the world on the same days, and usually involve a special mass and maybe a spot of decoration. In Goa, however, they're done differently.

Feasts are celebrated at different levels in the state. Some are large and celebrated state-wide, like the Feast of Saint Francis Xavier, or the Feast of St. John the Baptist. Others are celebrated at the village, town, or city level, like the feast of the patron saint of a church. Then there are *vaddo* (ward within a parish/town) level feasts, which are usually the feast of the patron saint of the chapel in that *vaddo*. And there are even smaller feasts to celebrate roadside shrines (known as *khuris* or crosses).

Every feast is celebrated a little differently. One of the most distinctive is the Feast of St. John the Baptist, more commonly known as São João. This quintessentially Goan celebration marks the baptism of Christ by John the Baptist. The feast takes

198

place during the peak of the monsoon, and it is said that rain on this day is good luck for the harvest season. It's a time when the wells are full, the landscape is lush and green, and most people have recovered from the inevitable flu-like symptoms brought on by the shift from the hot, humid summer to the cool and wet monsoon.

How is this celebrated, you ask? We jump into wells. Growing up, I was never allowed to jump in, but it was fun to watch. You'd have groups of shirtless men adorned with *kopels* (a kind of floral crown made from various vegetation) going from well to well singing a traditional São João song (yes, there's a special song for this feast) and jumping in, to cheers of "Viva São João!"

Ami Sogle zanvoim vortoutanv, chodda tempan bhetleanv,

Sao Joao-chem fest mhunnon ami mavoddea aileanv,

Mateak him kopelam ghalun udok navonk bhair sorleanv,

Aichea dissak voddle ami nokoi khuim pauleanv.

Chorus:

Sao Joao, Sao Joao gunvta mure vatt amkam dissonam,

Aicho dis urbecho konn konnak hansonam,

Choll-re pie-re tum illo ghe-re faleam kaim mevonam,

Oslim festam vorsak kiteak don pautti yenam.

Vhoddilanchea kaidea pormonem udok nataum bhaimchem,

Khoddegant fest hem amchem mavoddechem,

199

Pondra diss alchenoi hangache bhorench ami ghavchem

Choll atam Sao Joao vhoria maguir tem pouchem.

(Repeat Chorus)

Zanvoim ami festak aileanv mhunn vaddeant bobau poddla,

Mojea sasupain tin kouxe soro addla,

Tin kuddvanchim sandnam keleant ani dukor marla,

Sezarchea konsu manan ponos daddla.

(Repeat Chorus)

Translation (with poetic license to maintain the rhymes)

We've come to Mavoddea, the village's in-laws.

We've come after ages and Saint John's the cause,

Adorned with kopels, we're ready to bathe

And who knows where we'll be when the day starts to fade.

Chorus:

St. John, St John, we've lost our way

But we won't blame each other; it's an auspicious day.

Have a little drink, there'll be none tomorrow, I fear.

This feast should come at least twice a year.

We'll follow traditions and bathe in the well

Let's stay another fortnight, no bidding farewell

For now, let's celebrate the feast of Saint John

We can plan the details later; we have until dawn.

(Repeat Chorus)

The in-laws are here, it's the talk of the town

They butchered the piglet for us to wolf down

The father of my wife bought 3 kegs of feni

And the neighbour sent jackfruits, and sannas, so many.

(Repeat Chorus)

São João and the Feast of St. Francis Xavier are the only two feasts celebrated all over Goa. But São João is unique because every village celebrates the feast within its own community. There is no pilgrimage to any one place/church. And every village has its own way of celebrating it.

The most famous celebration of the feast is in the village of Siolim, where they have a boat parade.

A couple of tableaus at the boat parade (the people in the lower picture are wearing kopels)

Boats are transformed into intricate tableaus with themes varying from religion to sports to anything under the sun, and each boat in the parade carries a large *kopel*.

As the boats reach the end of the parade route, which is marked by a bridge across the river, they dock below the bridge, come ashore to a giant cross that stands right opposite the Siolim

Church, climb up the cross, and adorn it with the *kopel* they carried.

One of the participants placing a kopel on the cross

There's a lot of dancing, music, fanfare and crowds— not to mention the constant threat of rain, which is often realized— Goa's own version of "Wet n Wild".

Although this has nothing to do with the feast, the dish I most associate with São João is the egg drop curry that my mom would make. While every Goan is familiar with egg curry, egg drop curry is different and, in my opinion, much better. The difference is that, in the case of egg curry, the eggs are boiled and then added to the curry, whereas in egg drop curry, raw eggs are cracked into the boiling curry so that they get poached in the thick sauce. And if you like it, you can even ensure that the yolk remains a little runny.

Egg Drop Curry

Specific Equipment:

Mixer grinder or food processor

Ingredients (serves 3-4):

- 1 inch Ginger
- 4 cloves of Garlic
- 2 Shallots
- 5-7 Kashmiri Red Chillies
- 1 tsp Tamarind paste
- 500 ml (2 cups) Coconut Milk
- 1 tsp Black Peppercorns
- 1 tsp Cumin
- 1 tsp Coriander seeds
- 6 Eggs
- ½ + 1 cup Water
- 2 Tbsp Oil
- 1 tsp Salt or to taste

Method:

1. In a grinder or food processor, grind the ginger, garlic, shallots, chillies, tamarind, pepper, cumin and coriander into a fine paste. Add water as necessary.

2. Pour the oil into a pot on medium heat.

3. Once the oil is hot, add in the spice paste and stir-fry for a couple of minutes.

4. Add in the coconut milk and stir to combine.

5. Allow the curry to come to a boil and add the salt.

6. If the curry is too thick, add some more water to thin it out.

7. Taste and adjust the seasoning as required.

8. Once the curry is at a rolling boil, crack the eggs into the curry one at a time. Do not stir.

9. Cover the pot and turn off the heat.

Another of my creations that was inspired by São João is my Steak Tartare with Mushroom Cappuccino. Now this dish isn't for everyone, especially if you're averse to eating raw meat. But it is an instant favourite for those who can appreciate it. It's a slightly deviated steak tartare, seasoned with a bit of earthy cumin and coriander, with a slight tang from lime and a creamy richness from the mushroom cappuccino. It's best enjoyed spread on a crunchy slice of toasted bread.

Steak Tartare with Mushroom Cappuccino

Ingredients (serves 5-6):

For the steak tartare:

- 250 g Beef Round
- 1 Shallot, chopped fine
- 1 tsp finely chopped Coriander Leaves
- Salt to taste
- Freshly Cracked Black Pepper to taste
- ¼ tsp Cumin powder
- ¼ tsp Chilli powder

For the mushroom cappuccino:

- 250 g Mushrooms (a mix of button and oyster mushrooms works best, but use the type you like most), chopped fine
- 10 g Butter
- 1 tsp Olive Oil
- 1 inch Cinnamon stick
- 3 cloves of Garlic, finely minced
- 1 petal of Star Anise
- 1 tsp Cumin powder
- ½ tsp Turmeric powder
- 2 Tbsp Coriander powder

- 1 Tbsp Black Peppercorns

- 2 petals of Mace

- 2 pods of Cardamom, peeled

- 250 ml Coconut Milk

- 100 ml Water

Method:

Steak tartare:

1. Cut the beef into very small cubes (use a hand mincer if available).

2. Mix in the finely chopped shallots and the coriander.

3. Add the cumin powder, chilli powder, salt, and pepper to your taste, and mix.

Mushroom cappuccino:

1. Heat the butter and olive oil in a pan over low heat until the butter melts.

2. Add the garlic and sauté until it starts to brown.

3. Add the spices and stir a bit.

4. Add the mushrooms to the pan and stir-fry until they are tender and most of the liquid released dries up.

5. Add the coconut milk and water, and bring to a boil.

6. Cover and simmer for about 10 minutes.

7. Let it cool, and then fish out the star anise and cinnamon.

8. Blend the rest until it forms a smooth and creamy consistency (add water if necessary).

Assembly:

1. Use a cookie cutter or a ring mould to create a cylinder of the steak tartare. Remove the cookie cutter.

2. Pour the mushroom cappuccino into a small espresso mug and serve on the side.

3. Crack and separate an egg yolk and place the egg yolk on the tartare.

4. Serve with toast.

The Feast of St. Francis Xavier is celebrated by the whole of Goa, nay, the whole of India, on the 3rd of December. Every practising Goan Catholic makes it a point to attend one of the novena masses or the feast day mass. You have buses filled with pilgrims from all parts of India driving into the small village so that they can seek the blessings of the Saint.

St. Francis Xavier is the patron saint of Goa. *Goencho Saib* (Goa's Master), they call him, the Saint of Goa. Records prove that he was one of the main perpetrators of the inquisition in the state, writing letters to the then pope about locals worshipping idols which were "black as black can be and ugly to look at". Our *sussegado* attitude and over 400 years of servitude made us forgive and forget this era, and we fervently follow him.

When St. Francis Xavier died, and his body seemingly refused to remain in Malacca or return to Portugal, it was brought back to Goa, where it is paraded year after year in processions that celebrate the feast.

So well-preserved was his body that it is said that one pilgrim, in a fit of investigative self-authentication, bit off his toe to check if it was real, and rumour has it that it began to bleed. Since then, the body has been enclosed in an airtight case to protect him from other similarly inclined investigative chompers.

In recent years, the body leaves its residence in the Basilica de Bom Jesus at Old Goa only once every ten years, for the feast.

The whole village of Old Goa, outside the Cathedral, becomes one big fairground with vendors selling everything from toys and balloons to the traditional feast edibles – *kadiyo bodiyo* (a crunchy deep-fried chickpea batter finger dipped in either a ginger-jaggery or a plain sugar glaze), *jalebi* (a spiral shaped crisp & juicy sweet), *ladoos* (a spherical sweet), and *revdio* (another hard candy made of candied jaggery and coated with sesame seeds — similar to what I imagine a jawbreaker would be like, though I haven't tried one). Another famous feast food is *manna*, which is fried tapioca. It has a very mild flavour and is eaten for its crispy texture.

Besides these, you will also find the regular street fare of *choris pao* (Goan sausages stuffed in bread), *limbu soda* (fizzy limeade), and *cutlet pao* (a schnitzel-styled masala-marinated, semolina-coated steak, fried till well-done, and then some more, sandwiched within a loaf of bread — your choice of *pao*, *catre pao*, *unde* or *poie*, with a kind of coleslaw with vinegar instead of mayonnaise, and sometimes tomato ketchup).

Cutlet/Custulette Pao

Custulette Pao

Ingredients (serves 5):

For the salad:

- 1 cup Cabbage, shredded
- ½ Onion, finely sliced
- ¼ cup Carrots, shredded
- 2 Tbsp Vinegar (Coconut or Apple Cider)
- 1 Thai Green Chilli, minced

For the steak:

- 500 g Beef (eye of round), sliced into 100 g steaks
- 1 tsp Cumin
- 1 tsp ground Pepper
- ½ tsp Salt
- 6 cloves of Garlic, minced
- 1 inch Ginger, minced
- 1 tsp Red Chilli powder
- ¼ tsp Turmeric powder
- ⅛ tsp Cinnamon powder
- ⅛ tsp ground Cloves
- 1 Tbsp Cornflour
- ½ cup Semolina
- Juice of 1 Lime
- 5 Tbsp Oil
- 5 Goan Pao or Ciabatta Buns

Method:

The salad:

1. Place all the salad ingredients in a bowl and toss to combine. Taste and adjust seasoning.
2. You can also add some finely chopped coriander to the salad (optional).

3. Place the salad in the fridge until assembly.

The steak:

1. Beat the steaks between two pieces of parchment or plastic wrap until they are around 2 mm thick.

2. Combine the spices and salt with the ginger, garlic, and lime juice to form a paste.

3. Rub the paste onto the steaks and let them marinate in the fridge for at least an hour.

4. On a flat plate, mix the semolina and corn flour thoroughly.

5. Dredge each steak through the mixture, making sure it's evenly coated. Use light pressure to ensure the coating sticks.

6. Place a pan with the oil over high heat and wait until the oil begins to shimmer.

7. Gently place the steaks in the pan (do not crowd the pan).

8. Cook on each side until golden brown.

9. Remove the steaks from the pan and let them rest on a wire rack.

Assembly:

1. Cut the bread horizontally through the middle.

2. Spread with your choice of sauce, like mayonnaise or tomato ketchup (optional).

3. Place a steak on the lower half of the bread.

4. Place a helping of the salad on top of the steak.

5. Place the top half of the bread on top and serve as a sandwich.

Feast days were an intricate affair, regardless of whether it was a church feast, a chapel feast, or a *khurisa fest*. The format was always the same, with only the size and intensity of the celebration differing. The village/town/city feast was a big deal. As kids, we only got new clothes on three occasions: Christmas, Easter, and the village feast.

How do you know which feast to celebrate when there are multiple churches in larger villages, cities, and towns? Each church has a parish, which is a physical boundary, the occupants of which are members of that particular church. And each church has its own feast, for the saint that it is named after. But how is it decided which feast becomes the "flag bearer," the one that represents the whole town? Well, I believe the oldest or largest church gets the honour. For example, there are at least three churches (maybe more) within the city of Margao. The Holy Spirit church, which is the oldest of them, represents Margao. And hence, when one uses the term "Margao feast", they are referring to the feast celebrated at the Holy Spirit Church.

Feast days are extra special occasions. For one, it's a school holiday, and important enough for those working to take the day off. The day starts early, and after a quick *chao* or coffee, you get dressed in your brand-new clothes. The whole family then goes to church together, usually for the high mass, which used to be at 8 a.m. This mass goes on for two to three hours, depending on the celebrant. My family never attended the high mass. We usually went for the earliest mass, which was at 6 a.m. That way, we had plenty of time to get groceries, get back home, and cook the feast meal, which would be consumed at lunch. We were holy, but not to the detriment of practicality.

As children, we saw the feast as an hour of suffering (through mass), followed by a day of merriment. Like I mentioned earlier, the area around the church would turn into fairgrounds with multiple things to do. There were games, some shows, rides, food vendors, furniture vendors, etc. There'd be a whole bunch of local vendors who'd brought their wares to sell. It was a time for the church to make some money, and they would use every means at their disposal: rent the fairgrounds, hold a raffle, pin favours onto churchgoers lapels, and, of course, the donation boxes.

I loved the favours as a kid, and I don't know why. The favours, as we called them, were simply crepe paper flowers made by volunteers, which they pinned onto your lapel for a donation. It was just a small donation of maybe 1-2 rupees, but the favour on the lapel of my brand-new shirt made me feel important somehow. Never mind that everyone had one; it was still special. Maybe it gave me some sense of belonging to the community, or some indication of support for my church, I don't know, but I felt proud to wear it. And I'd wear that damn paper flower on my lapel all day long.

After mass, our parents would head to the market to buy groceries for the feast meal, and they'd leave us with some money to enjoy the fair.

We were mostly unsupervised, but being within the village, there were plenty of people who kept an eye on us and would report us to our parents if needed. The fair was full of fun for kids. We enjoyed playing games like ring toss, where you had to throw a ring around an object to win that object; or ping pong slots, where you rolled ping pong balls down an inclined board into numbered slots at the end, and won prizes when the scores added up to specific totals. The prizes could be something stupid, like a bar of soap, or the more coveted items like cash, soda, candy, and sometimes toys.

Speaking of toys, the feast was also a great place to buy some really old-school toys, from steam-powered little putt-putt boats to friction cars with spark siren lights. They were cheap toys made from old repurposed metal tins with sharp edges and cheap plastic parts. The kind that would probably get today's parents up on a tizzy. But back then, parenting wasn't as protective. If you cut yourself on the sharp metal, you learned to be more careful. Nothing a few band-aids, a little antiseptic, and maybe a tetanus shot couldn't fix.

But back to the toys. Those toys were how I learned science. The putt-putt boat taught me Newton's 3rd law of motion, the friction cars taught me about flywheels and potential energy, and also that friction can cause sparks, which is super cool!

After a few hours at the fair, we'd head home, where the guests, our relatives from other villages, would start arriving. The snacks served would be the usual croquettes, chutney sandwiches, patties, and masala nuts. Adults would be served drinks, usually whiskey or beers, and we kids would get soft drinks, Thums up (an Indian cola), or more likely Njal, which was a local drink company.

There'd be a lot going on, and the line between guests and hosts would get blurry. Everyone chipped in, helping with the cooking, bartending, serving, or clean-up. The older kids would take on babysitting responsibilities, making sure the younger ones weren't doing anything too naughty or dangerous. There was what seemed like an endless supply of everything – snacks, drinks, toys. Once the food was ready, everyone would gather around the dining table, which was laid out buffet-style — there were far too many of us to actually sit at it.

Christmas Buffet

We'd say grace together, then begin serving ourselves. This was usually a very late lunch (hence the copious amounts of snacks), often at around three or four in the afternoon. And the food — oh, the food — was plentiful.

I've noticed a big cultural difference between North American celebratory meals and Goan ones. North America focuses on one main dish and a few sides, while in Goa, we have multiple mains and a few sides. A typical feast meal would include *pulao*, *sorpotel*, beef or tongue roast, either a roast or a curry chicken, a vegetable dish, a salad (usually an Olivier or tuna salad), fried fish or shrimp/prawns, and finally a dessert, sometimes two, the most common being caramel custard and jelly.

The guests would leave after lunch, which meant it was clean-up time – dishes, floors, and everything in between. The house, which had transformed from a home into a party venue, now had to be turned back into a home again. This involved rearranging furniture, bringing out the delicate show-pieces that had been hidden away for fear of breakage (with kids running wild through the house), and hunting down cutlery and crockery that somehow migrated to every corner — even the garden. Then, and only then, would the hosts finally rest. We'd change into comfy home clothes and sit back to relive the day's events — read: exchange the freshest gossip.

That evening, we'd usually go back to the fair and have a light dinner, usually cutlet *pao* or *choris pao*. We'd try our luck at another round of games, and maybe go on a few rides, before buying some *chone* (a collective term used to describe a mixture of roasted chickpeas, peanuts, and white peas) and maybe some *kadiyo bodiyo*.

The chapel feast (*kopela fest*) and the feasts of the crosses (*khurisa fest*) were celebrated on a much smaller scale. You had the usual decorations, prayers, and, of course, food, but no fairgrounds. At chapel feasts, food would be served to all attendees, right outside the chapel. Most commonly, it would be a pre-plated *pulao* with a chicken or goat *xacuti* and some beef stew on the side.

Xacuti

Specific Equipment:

Dry grinder

Mixer grinder or food processor

Ingredients (serves 10):

- 7 Kashmiri Red Chillies
- 1 inch Cinnamon stick
- 2 petals of Star Anise
- 1 tsp Cumin seeds
- 1 tsp Turmeric powder
- 2 Tbsp Coriander seeds
- 1 Tbsp Black Peppercorns
- 2 petals of Mace

- 2 pods of Cardamom
- 1 Tbsp Poppy seeds
- 200 g Fresh Grated Coconut
- 5 Cloves of Garlic
- 1 inch Ginger
- 2 Shallots
- 1 tsp Tamarind paste
- 1 Kg Meat (traditionally goat or beef diced into 1 inch cubes, or chicken bone-in curry cut)
- 1 ½ tsp Salt
- 3-4 cups Water

Method:

1. Season the meat with the salt and set it aside in the fridge.

2. In a pan over low heat, roast each of the following spices separately until they are aromatic: chillies, cinnamon, star anise, cumin, turmeric, coriander, pepper, mace, cardamom, and poppy seeds.

3. Place all the spices in the jar of a dry grinder and grind them into a fine powder.

4. Set the powder aside.

5. Using the same pan over low heat, roast the coconut, ginger, garlic, and shallots until they begin to caramelize.

6. Place the roasted ingredients and tamarind into the grinder/food processor.

7. Pour about ½ to 1 cup of water, and grind into a wet paste.

8. Add the dry powder to the paste and stir to combine.

9. Place a heavy-bottomed pot over medium heat and pour the paste into the pot.

10. Bring the gravy to a boil adding water as required.

11. Add the meat to the pot.

12. Cover the pot and let it come to a boil.

13. Simmer for about 15-20 minutes.

14. Taste the gravy and adjust the seasoning.

15. Serve with rice or *pao/poie*.

The word chapel can be misleading. While by definition a chapel is "a Christian place of prayer and worship that is usually relatively small", there do exist chapels that are bigger than churches, accommodating over 400 people. The chapel in my village was small, comparable in size, shape, and structure to a kind of walled gazebo, or bandstand, if you will.

In fact, after I watched that iconic coming-of-age dance in "The Sound of Music" with Liesel and Rolfe, the young, soon-to-be-eighteen, almost-Nazi messenger boy, I could imagine myself leaping from bench to bench along the Chapel walls. These benches lined the inside walls that supported the only external feature that distinguished the hexagon-shaped chapel from a gazebo: its steeple and bell tower. Of course, one bench was glaringly missing, replaced by the pulpit and the altar, with its pillars, intricately carved with grapevines, and arches and domes sheltering numerous cherubs and likenesses of saints. It would have been beautiful if it hadn't been plated in gaudy gold, due to which the painstakingly hand-carved designs lost their depth and appeared to meld into one giant textured structure.

Anyway, our chapel could barely accommodate 50 people, even with attendees standing. So the family celebrating the feast would hire a bunch of metal folding chairs—blue seats and backrests with "Costas" stencilled in white, and light aqua green frames. You'd see these chairs at most occasions, weddings, house-warming parties, village dances, tiatrs (folk plays) and anything that called for extra seating. It feels like there was only one provider of chairs for the whole of Goa, back then. The chairs would be placed outside the front of the chapel, and there would be a celebration of the Eucharist on a temporary altar constructed outside, followed by food and drinks. Caterers would bring in large vessels (big enough to fit a 5-year-old child) full of food, portion it onto plates that would be carried 20-30 on a large tray held between two waiters. You can still witness this at many Goan events. The waiters would distribute the plates, supervised by a member of the family celebrating the feast, who ensured everyone was served (and served only once – you can't have people eating twice when you pay per plate). Portions were generous, yet wastage was minimal, because, as our mothers told us, there were so many people starving around the world. How would stuffing ourselves with food alleviate their suffering or make their suffering worth it? I'm not sure, because it was never explained, and we were too obedient (read as: scared of the ass whopping that would be gained by "back-answering") to ask why, what or how.

Another feast-like religious celebration among the Catholics is "Our Lady" or *Saibini*. This is a ritual that takes place sometime around October-November. It involves a statue of the Virgin Mary travelling from household to household. The statue spends one night in each household, during which some prayers are said as friends, family, and neighbours gather together to worship. The prayers are usually followed by some snacks for the worshippers, the most popular of which is *chone* (boiled chickpeas with slices of coconut).

Saibini Chone

Ingredients (serves 4):

- 1 cup Chickpeas, soaked for 8 hours
- ¼ cup fresh Coconut meat, cut into ¼ inch dice
- 1 Tbsp Salt
- 2 cups of Water

Method:

1. Strain the chickpeas, discarding the water in which they were soaking.

2. Add the chickpeas into a heavy-bottomed pot with the water and salt (make sure that the water is at least 1 inch more than the level of the chickpeas in the pot).

3. Bring the pot to a boil and let it simmer for 30 minutes to an hour, until the chickpeas are soft enough to eat.

4. Strain the chickpeas, add in the coconut and mix it up.

5. Serve warm or cold, adding salt if necessary.

Chapter 15:
'Tis the Season

If you live along the coast, conversations almost always revolve around "the season" — "The season has been really bad this year, but off-season was good", "Everyone is saying the season is bad, but look at the number of foreigners around". The term "season," used by itself in Goa, refers to the tourist season.

Back when hippies still roamed the world preaching free love and "sticking it to the man", Goa had a distinct time of the year when these flower power seekers of spiritual nirvana (ironically, while listening to them) found their promised land. A land where the sun always shone, the breeze was always cool, and the grass was, well, as grass is, green with five to seven leaves and smokable. This lasted from late October to early May and was christened "the season".

"The season" is when Goa really is "as seen on TV" – beaches with shacks serving overpriced seafood and renting out deck-chairs, clear blue skies speckled with brightly coloured parachutes carrying parasailing tourists, beat shows (evening concerts with multiple bands and, of course, food and drinks), balls, Christmas, New Year, the Carnival parade, and, the less popular but much more awesome, *Shigmo* parade (with larger-than-life floats depicting stories from various Hindu religious epics and myths). It's crowded, it's loud, it's energetic, but oxymoronically, it's still peaceful and tranquil. You can go from relaxing on a deck bed with a chilled beer, or whatever cocktail draws your fancy, by your side, to an all-night rager in a couple of hours. It is, whatever you want it to be; you just need to find that little pocket that you fit in.

For me, the season begins with *Narakasura* (a part of Goan Diwali Celebrations) and ends with *urrack* (the lovely alcoholic schnapps made from the juice of the cashew apple), with a whole lot in between.

Narakasura: Goa's own Hellboy

Come Diwali, in most parts of India, you'll find families lighting *diyas* (oil lamps) and fireworks to celebrate the festival of light. In most parts of India, they're celebrating the return of the exiled Rama to Ayodhya. But Goa prides itself in being different from India. While Goans also celebrate the return of Rama, the prime focus of Diwali tends to be the defeat of Narakasura.

Now I'm no theologian, and I'm sure there will be a number of people who will dispute that last sentence. But I'm calling it as I see it. In a true and proper practice of Hinduism, the prime focus of the festival of Diwali is probably the *pujas* (ritual worship) offered to the Goddesses Lakshmi and Saraswati, but like Christmas outshines Easter—even though Easter is supposed to be the more significant of the two—in Goa, the defeat of Narakasura by Lord Krishna overshadows the rest of Diwali by far.

Naraka (Naraka was his name, and the *asura* got added on because he was a demon - *asura* is Sanskrit for "demon"), as per

'Vedic' texts, was a good guy until the usual combination of power and bitterness of rejection caused him to go bad. He ruled the whole of the earth, and the heavens too. Even the mighty Indra, the God of Gods, India's equivalent of Zeus (a rainbow is called an *Indradhanush,* which translates to "Indra's Bow", for his arrows, which I assume are lightning bolts), was afraid of him and left the heavens.

The only one who could end his reign was his father, Vishnu, a part of the Hindu trinity of Brahma, Vishnu and Shiva — the creator, the preserver and the destroyer, respectively. Vishnu had already granted Narakasura's mother a boon: her son would enjoy a long reign. After what Vishnu deemed "a long reign" (this is why you have to be specific with your requests), he decided to intervene. He reincarnated — as he often did, as Krishna, known for stealing butter, flirting with milkmaids (probably in attempts to get more butter), and stealing their clothes while they bathed in the river — the origin of "boys will be boys" – one of the many filthy adages spewed by male chauvinists, and Indian leaders in particular, to justifying crimes against women.

Krishna grew up and eventually waged war against the demon king. After what one can only imagine was an intense battle, he killed Narakasura, and it is this victory that is celebrated in Goa on the day before Diwali.

The battle and the end of Narakasura's reign are celebrated with great pomp and show. Kids and youth together build effigies of the demon king, and the government organizes a parade to showcase them, complete with prizes awarded for the best ones. Included is usually a short enactment of the kill, performed in the form of a dance to the beat of traditional drums called *dhols*. It's an experience I highly recommend. At midnight, the effigies are set ablaze.

An Effigy of Narakasura

The effigies get more intricate and elaborate every year. In the early 1990s, they were simple life-sized effigies. Today, some tower at 30 feet, and feature mechanized and robotic elements.

The day after Narakasura marks my favourite part of Diwali, and what I like to call "Diwali brunch". You visit your Hindu friends on this day to wish them a happy Diwali and enjoy the flavourful vegetarian spread prepared by their family. There's beaten rice (*faw* or *poha*) served in different forms — some sweet, some savoury, and some crunchy. Unfortunately, I never bothered to learn all the individual dish names, but I'll just put it down to Shakespeare's rose; a dish, after all, tastes just as good by any other name.

The pièce de résistance for me is the *ambade* (hog plum) curry. Oh, this wonderfully sweet, sour and spicy, beautifully textured curry-chutney crossover, spiced and tempered with mustard seeds and curry leaves, is heavenly. For those who haven't tasted it, the *ambade* is a sour plum with a large pit. It hardly has any flesh on it, but it is one of those things that Goan children love, along with unripe mangoes and bilimbis. We'd enjoy these nature's treats with a mixture of salt and chilli powder, resulting in a salty-sour taste with a spicy finish. I guarantee that anyone who has ever had this deliciousness is salivating right now.

Ambade curry is a truly delightful dish. It can be eaten on its own or with bread, but I love it best when slathered generously over *faw/poha*. The combination is heavenly, the almost crunchy, al dente texture of the flattened rice paired with the sweet-sour richness of the curry feels like being wrapped in your mother's comforting hug.

Hog plums aren't easily available outside India; in fact, even in India, they're rare. You can substitute any sour fruit in the curry, and I'm sure it'll taste just as good. In fact, Goa has a similar curry made of unripe mangoes.

Ok, enough stalling, here's the recipe:

Faw/Poha

Ingredients (serves 2-3):

- 1 cup Beaten Flat-rice
- ¼ tsp Turmeric powder
- 1 tsp Mustard seeds
- A pinch of Asafoetida
- 1 Green Chilli, chopped fine
- 1 Onion or 2 Shallots, chopped fine
- 2 Tbsp Split Mung Beans or Split Chickpeas
- 10 Curry Leaves
- 1 Tbsp Oil
- Salt to taste
- Coriander to garnish
- Lime wedges for serving

Method:

1. Rinse the flattened rice under running water until it becomes soft (it should lose its stiffness but not become mushy).

2. Pour the oil into a pan and place it on medium-high heat.

3. Once the oil is hot, add the mustard seeds. They should begin to splutter.

4. Once the popping slows to about 1 second between pops, add in the split mung beans/chickpeas and cook until they start to brown.

5. Add the curry leaves, asafoetida and turmeric, and stir until fragrant or until the curry leaves start to blister.

6. Add the onions and sauté until they are translucent.

7. Season with salt.

8. Add in the chilli and the flattened rice.

9. Stir the mixture to coat the flattened rice.

10. Cover and let it steam on low heat for about 5 minutes, stirring intermittently.

11. Garnish with the chopped coriander and serve with a lime wedge.

Ambade (Hog Plum) Curry

Specific Equipment:

Mixer grinder or food processor

Ingredients (serves 5-6):

- 500 g Ambade (Hog Plums), washed and peeled
- 300 g Grated Coconut
- 100 ml (½ cup) Coconut Milk
- 2 tsp Mustard Seeds
- 3 Tbsp Coconut Jaggery or Unrefined Palm Sugar
- 10 Curry Leaves
- 6-7 Kashmiri Red Chillies
- 2 tsp Salt
- 1 tsp Turmeric powder

Method:

1. Place the hog plums in a bowl.
2. Mix the salt and jaggery.
3. Rub the salt and jaggery mixture into the plums and leave them to marinate for a couple of hours.
4. Grind the coconut, chillies, and turmeric to form a paste. You can add water to aid the grinding process (if needed).

5. Pour the oil into a pan and place it over medium-high heat.

6. Once the oil is hot, add the mustard seeds. They should begin to splutter.

7. Once the popping slows to about 1 second between pops, add in the curry leaves.

8. Once the curry leaves begin to blister, add in the ground paste.

9. The hog plums, which were marinating in the salt-jaggery mixture, will have given out juices, making the marinade a thick syrup. Add this marinade and the hog plums into the pan along with the coconut milk, and let it come to a boil.

10. Once boiling, reduce the heat to low and let it simmer for 10 minutes, until the hog plums are tender.

Moong Gathi

Specific Equipment:

Mixer grinder or food processor

Ingredients:

- ½ cup Fresh Grated Coconut

- ½ tsp Turmeric powder

- 2 Green Chillies, roughly chopped

- 1 tsp Tamarind

- 2 Tbsp Oil

- 1 tsp Mustard Seeds
- A pinch of Asafoetida, or 1 tsp each of minced Garlic and Ginger
- 8 Fresh Curry Leaves
- 1 Onion, sliced
- 1 cup Mung Beans
- 1½ tsp Salt

Method:

1. Soak the mung beans in water for 24 hours.
2. Grind the coconut, turmeric, chillies and tamarind together in the grinder/food processor with a little water until it forms a smooth paste.
3. Drain the mung beans and transfer them to a pot.
4. Add salt and water to cover the contents.
5. Boil until the beans are tender, then drain and set aside.
6. Pour the oil into a pan and place it on medium-high heat.
7. Once the oil is hot, add the mustard seeds. They should begin to splutter.
8. Once the popping slows to about 1 second between pops, add in the curry leaves and the asafoetida (or ginger and garlic) and onions.
9. Sauté until the onions start to caramelize.

10. Add the paste from step 2, and bring it to a boil.

11. Add in the mung beans and let them simmer for a few minutes.

12. Take off the heat and serve over rice or with *chapatis*.

Christmas

It's the most wonderful time of the year! Christmas is big in Goa. The most beautiful thing about the Goa I grew up in was that it was a true cultural mosaic—everyone participated in everything. As Christians, we joined in Diwali celebrations, helped build floats for *Shigmo*, and shared the communal biryani for Eid. Similarly, our neighbours, regardless of their faith, joined us in the celebration of feasts and festivals. It wasn't uncommon to see people of other religions attend the novenas of St. Francis Xavier, the feast mass, and even Christmas balls.

As is in most parts of the world, Christmas was one of our favourite times as kids. It might have been so for the adults, too, if not for the stress that came along with it. Most families (and by "family" I mean grandparents and all their descendants) in Goa had a few members working abroad, either in the Gulf, the Middle Eastern countries of Saudi Arabia, UAE, Qatar, Oman, Bahrain and Kuwait, or on ships (either the merchant navy or passenger liners). They'd all return home for Christmas, and the house would be packed. As everywhere else in the world, family can be... complicated. Christmas was a time when feasting and fighting went hand in hand. Old wounds were reopened, and peacemakers worked overtime. One moment, everyone was celebrating and singing together, and the next, a fight would break out. It was insane and unbelievable, but believe me, it was real.

There's a lot of resentment and repressed anger in most Goans. Some of it stems from childhood trauma, some from a culture of constant comparison, where children are measured against the achievements of their siblings, cousins and peers, and some from the daily frustrations of life in a developing nation entangled in red tape and corruption.

Aside from that, it was a wonderful time. My family would try to stay within our own little nucleus for peace of mind, but it was rare that we were left alone.

Back when I was in school, the Christmas holidays began on the 19th of December — Goa Liberation Day — the day that Goa was either liberated from the Portuguese or invaded by India, depending on whom you ask. In my house, the Christmas season began on this day.

We would start by cleaning the house and changing the upholstery, the cushion covers, tablecloths, curtains, everything had to be replaced with their festive version. That alone was a whole day's affair. You'd think we'd be spared as kids, but no such luck. Because of our small size and flexibility, we were tasked with all the climbing and crouching into hard-to-reach places. The toughest and most dreaded, job for me was scrubbing away the algae that had built up on the exterior walls during the monsoons. Pressure washers were unheard of, so I had to tackle it by hand with a wire brush. Since our house was fairly large, it would take me the entire day.

Next came the decorations. The house had to be adorned with Christmas lights, tinsel, streamers and the like, even though none of it would actually be lit until after midnight mass on the 24th. One of the most important decorations was the star, symbolizing the Star of Bethlehem. Every celebrating family had one either hanging from the roof or, if you lived in a flat (apartment or condo), balcony, with a light bulb in it.

The most intricate decoration, however, was the crib, which is what we called the nativity tableau that was essential in every home. During the years that we lived in a flat (apartment), I built small cribs out of cardboard and straw, and carefully arranged those absolutely ugly clay figurines – the wise men, shepherds, Holy Family, farm animals, and the angel Gabriel – that were sold in the market at Christmas time. These figurines were poorly made, never fired in a kiln, and simply painted over with bright oil paints. They were ugly and broke easily, but with no other alternatives back then, they're all we had to use.

There were other cribs, though, the ones built to impress. You still see these works of art at Christmas, growing more elaborate with each passing year. Some are life-sized creations, others involve mechanized elements, and a few take on flights of fantasy, incorporating Santa Claus or pop culture characters from movies and current events. We Goans, take our art seriously, and we make sure it stays socially relevant.

Every parish would host a crib competition, with a prize for the best creation. The prize was modest, wouldn't cover the cost of building the crib, but the bragging rights made it all worthwhile.

In towns, store fronts were adorned with banners that wished everyone "Season's Greetings" or the classic "Merry Christmas and Happy New Year". Pop-up shops appeared everywhere selling Christmas decorations, while the markets glowed with colourful lights and overflowed with stalls selling Christmas sweets, a healthy mix of traditional ones like *doce, bolinhas, batica, dodol, pinagre, ghos, bebinca,* modern ones like marzipan fruits, jujubes, rose cookies, date rolls, milk creams, and Christmas cake (both traditional and modern).

Christmas traditions vary from family to family and even person to person. When I was in university, semester exams were always around Christmas. That meant missing out on most of the celebrations to study and prepare for lab work and theory papers.

I once met a family, travelling in the same bus as me, who were headed to Nashik. While Nashik is the primary wine growing region in India, located in Maharashtra, a few 700 km from Goa, it is also home to a shrine dedicated to the Infant Jesus, believed to be very powerful in granting wishes and miracles. It was this family's tradition to travel there every Christmas Eve to pray and light a candle at the shrine.

My family's traditions didn't include anything that elaborate. Ours was simple: attend early morning mass, have Christmas sweets for breakfast, prep for lunch, and sit down to a late lunch — an enormous spread accompanied by copious amounts of alcohol. After lunch came the clean-up, and that was the day.

Dinner was usually skipped altogether, or replaced with a light meal — a sandwich or a soup. Carols played all day long, which I'd like to say was fun, but in all honesty, they'd been on repeat in my house since the beginning of Advent, and so by Christmas Day, I was well and truly over it.

The real parties in Goa, when I was younger, were the dinner dances held on Christmas Eve. My parents would attend these and dance the night away. The event would typically start around 9 or 10 p.m., and the music wouldn't stop until 5 or 6 in the morning. So my parents would be out all night, only to meet us (my grandmom and me) directly for the 6 a.m. mass at the church.

By the time I was in my teens, midnight mass had grown popular, and Christmas Eve dances would start only after it concluded, around 1 a.m. Midnight mass was a big event, and every church celebrated it a little differently. Schools run by the clergy would transform their playgrounds into makeshift arenas to accommodate the faithful. Imagine a soccer field filled with rows of chairs facing a dais, on which stood a temporary altar. The chairs were the usual Costa chairs (metal folding chairs bearing the rental company's name — Costa). The sound system was usually provided by Kane Radio in South Goa or Asis in North Goa. There'd be well over a thousand chairs, and yet you'd see people standing. Mass at Loyola's school began at 11:30 p.m., but you had to be there at 10 to get a good seat.

When I went with my family, we'd arrive at 10 and sit together. Later, I preferred going with friends, as it allowed us to show up later and claim spots in the school corridors instead. The corridors had several advantages. We'd be out of the view of the priests, chaperones and parents, which meant we could chat freely with friends. We'd sneak glances at our crushes to admire their outfits, or, if we were lucky, find our crush standing right beside us, giving us a rare chance to talk to them.

As soon as mass ended, we'd rush down from the corridors to meet the few key people who would vouch for us to our parents. Goa is a small place, and if you didn't greet the community busybodies, it would be reported: "I didn't see your son at midnight mass for Christmas. He didn't come to wish me." or "I saw your son after mass, and he didn't even come to greet me."

We'd then hop on our scooters (little mopeds we called "bikes" in Goa) and ride off to a Christmas dance or a party, where we'd spend the rest of the night and the early hours. We'd get home around 7 a.m., and grab a few winks before joining the family for Christmas lunch.

clockwise from left: **Pulao, Sorpotel & Roulade**

Christmas lunch was similar to a feast lunch, only on a grander scale. Since we didn't eat meat every day at home, the spread had to include every kind imaginable.

There'd be beef, usually in the form of a roast, or more likely, roast tongue, or my personal favourite: a stew.

Pork came as a roast suckling pig, alongside *sorpotel*, which deserves its own section and will get one further down.

Chicken would be the most experimented with, of the meats. The traditional preparations were roast or *cafreal*, but my grandmother and mother often tried out different recipes and ideas. One of my favourites was a deviled chicken my mom made — a recipe I've never managed to replicate despite having her handwritten recipe (which I've concluded was more for her interpretation than to be followed exactly). I hope to recreate it someday, but until then, it remains lost.

Fish was always on the table, too. Either my dad's whole fish poached in white wine or semolina-crusted fish.

There'd be an assortment of bread: *pao*, *poie*, sliced bread, and sometimes *sannas* — those heavenly steamed coconut rice cakes that are sweet, savory and fluffy, and pair perfectly with the *sorpotel*.

Vegetables appeared in salads, usually a Russian (Olivier) salad, but my mom, ever the voice of healthy eating, would insist on a leafy green salad to ensure we got some extra fibre.

Rice came in the form of a *pulao*, either made with shrimp/prawns, *tisreo* (clams) or vegetables (peas or mixed vegetables).

Finally, for dessert, my grandmother would have spent an entire night at the bakery baking her delicious layered *bebinca*, often called the queen of Goan desserts. There would also be all the other Goan Christmas sweets, which we'd also had for breakfast earlier.

After lunch, we'd rest for a while before heading out to the Christmas ball, another night of merriment. Although this event had a more formal vibe, towards the latter part of the night, it would transform into a more contemporary party with a DJ or band playing the latest hits. Dinner was usually had at the ball itself, or we'd slip out for a late night *roce omelette*.

Russian Salad (Salad Olivier)

Ingredients (serves 4-6):

- 1 cup of Carrots, boiled, peeled and medium diced (¼ inch)
- ½ cup of Potatoes, boiled, peeled and medium diced (¼ inch)
- 1 cup of Green Peas
- ½ cup of Apples, peeled and medium diced (¼ inch)
- 1 cup of Mayonnaise
- 4 Eggs boiled, peeled and cut into quarters
- 2 Tbsp Parsley or Coriander, finely chopped
- Fresh cracked pepper to taste

Method:

1. In a large salad bowl, mix all the ingredients (except for the eggs and coriander/parsley) well to ensure everything is well coated in the mayonnaise.
2. Place the quartered eggs on top.
3. Garnish with the coriander/parsley.

Chicken Cafreal

Chicken Cafreal

Ingredients (serves 4):

- 500 g Chicken, bone-in and skin-on (I prefer using only legs and thighs, but go with what you prefer)
- 1 Onion, sliced into rings

For the spice paste:

- 6 cloves of Garlic (or 1 Tbsp Garlic paste)
- 1 inch Ginger (or ½ Tbsp Ginger paste)
- 1 tsp Ground Black Pepper
- 1 tsp Cumin
- 1 Tbsp Coriander seeds

- 3 whole Cloves
- 1 inch Cinnamon stick (or a pinch of powdered Cinnamon)
- 1 Tbsp Vinegar (Coconut or Apple Cider)
- 1 tsp Salt
- 1 cup Coriander leaves
- 5 Green Chillies
- 1½ tsp Sugar

Method:

The spice paste:

1. Grind all the spice paste ingredients to form a smooth paste with the consistency of a chutney.
2. Score the chicken up to the bone with a sharp knife. Make the scores about 2 inches apart.
3. Rub the spice paste all over the chicken and into the scores.
4. Cover and refrigerate for 2-8 hours, the longer the better.
5. Take the chicken out of the marinade and keep the marinade aside for later.

Cooking the chicken — Method 1: Barbecue

1. Start the barbecue and bring the coals to a glowing red (400°F).

2. Grill the chicken over the open flame of the barbecue until it gets some char.

3. Set the chicken on the cooler side of the grill or on a higher rack, and close the lid.

4. Cook for about 20 minutes or until an internal temperature of 165°F is reached.

5. Pour the remaining marinade into a skillet.

6. Add a little water and bring the marinade to a boil over low heat.

7. Let the marinade simmer for at least 15 minutes before taking it off the heat.

Cooking the chicken — Method 2: Oven

1. Preheat the oven to 400°F.

2. Place the chicken on a wire rack and into the oven for 10 minutes.

3. In a separate oven-safe dish, pour in the marinade.

4. Take the chicken off the wire rack and place it in the dish with the marinade.

5. Reduce the oven temperature to 350°F.

6. Cover the chicken and dish with aluminium foil.

7. Place it into the oven for another 50-80 minutes or until an internal temperature of 165°F is reached at the thickest portion.

Cooking the chicken — Method 3: Stove Top

1. Pour 1 Tbsp of oil into a large skillet and place it over medium-high heat.

2. Place the chicken in the hot skillet and let it brown, turning it over at regular intervals so that it doesn't burn.

3. Reduce the heat to medium-low and add in the marinade with a little (up to 4 Tbsp) of water.

4. Cover the skillet with a lid.

5. When the liquid starts bubbling, leave it to simmer for about 15 minutes or until the chicken reads an internal temperature of 165°F.

Plating:

1. Garnish the chicken with raw onion rings and serve it with a little of the simmered gravy/marinade.

2. The dish is usually served with fries or little roast potatoes, bread and a wedge of lime.

Roulade

Roulade is another very traditional Goan-Portuguese recipe that finds itself at the Christmas table. Traditionally, the roulade that my grandmother made consisted of thin slices of beef stuffed with *choris*, green onion, carrot, and potato rolled into a tight cylinder and then poached in a thick, spiced gravy. This method of cooking works well for Indian beef, which is usually tougher and leaner, and needs a longer cook time. In North

America and Europe, however, an oven-roast roulade works better.

Specific Equipment:

Mixer grinder or food processor, or mortar and pestle

Meat mallet

Ingredients (serves 4-5):

- 500 g Beef Tenderloin (or striploin), cut into thin slices (between 3-5mm)
- 1 tsp Cumin seeds
- 1 tsp Black Peppercorns
- 2 whole Cloves
- 1 inch Cinnamon stick
- 1 Tbsp Garlic paste
- ½ Tbsp Ginger paste
- 1 - 1½ tsp salt (to taste)
- Juice of 1 lime
- 10 links of Goan *choris*, removed from the casing/skin
- 120 g Potatoes, julienned (shoestring or up to ¼" thick)
- 120 g Carrots, julienned
- 1 bunch Green Onions, julienned

Method:

1. Grind the cumin, pepper, cloves and cinnamon into a fine powder using a dry grinder/food processor or a mortar and pestle.

2. Transfer the powder into a medium-sized bowl.

3. Add the salt, ginger, garlic and the lime juice to form the marinade for the meat.

4. Take each piece of beef, place it between two sheets of parchment paper or cellophane wrap and use a meat mallet to flatten the beef into a thin, even sheet of about 2 mm thickness.

5. Coat the flattened beef slices with the marinade.

6. Cover the bowl (containing the beef slices) and let it rest in the fridge for 1 to 8 hours.

7. Pour a litre of water into a saucepan and bring it to a boil.

8. Blanch the carrots and potatoes in the water for about 1 minute, then set them aside to cool.

9. Set the oven to 350°F.

10. Take a slice of beef and lay it flat on a cutting board or other clean surface.

11. Place a small amount of *choris*, one piece of green onion, one piece of potato and one piece of carrot along one of the shorter ends of the beef.

12. Wrap the beef around the filling ingredients and roll it as tightly as possible so that it forms a tight cylinder.

13. Place the cylinder into the baking dish with the open flap on the bottom, so that it doesn't open. A small baking dish is recommended to ensure there's no space between the rolls for them to move.

14. Repeat with each of the remaining slices of beef, arranging them as close together as possible.

15. Pour the remaining marinade over the rolls and cover the baking dish with aluminium foil.

16. Place the covered baking dish into the preheated oven and bake for around 20 minutes.

17. Serve with *pulao*.

Sorpotel

Now, let's talk about *sorpotel*. It's the dish that demands the most technique in Goan cuisine and is usually the piéce de résistance at a meal. As mentioned before, the key difference between Eastern and Western cuisines lies in the concept of a main ingredient. Western cuisines often revolve around a star ingredient, complemented by a few side dishes. In Eastern cuisine, however, we don't focus on a star ingredient; we proudly offer up a star dish.

It's the way we eat that shapes this difference. In India, for instance, we usually start with what you could call a "bread course", where you serve yourself some bread plate along with the more fluid dishes; curries or stews, and use the bread to soak them up like a sponge. Next comes the "rice course": you pile on the rice and serve yourself the thicker gravies *cafreal*, *xacuti*, *vindalho*. At this point, you also serve yourself a bit of everything else at the table, and eat it together.

The harsh reality about most Eastern cuisine is that the protein doesn't really matter. If you build a good gravy or sauce, you can drop almost any protein into it, and it will taste great. That's why butter chicken and *paneer makhani* (the cottage cheese version of butter chicken) are essentially the same dish, with only a slight difference in flavour and texture.

This holds true for much of Goan cuisine as well. A fish curry, shrimp/prawn curry or egg curry shares remarkably similar flavours. But there are also dishes that stand apart — ones that rely on technique and demand a specific protein. And the best example of that is *sorpotel*.

Sorpotel is usually made a week before the day it is meant to be served, and each day, it's brought to a boil and then cooled rapidly, allowing the flavours to mingle and deepen as the sharpness of the vinegar mellows, resulting in a quite complex flavour. The process is essentially a kind of pickling, which is why *sorpotel* can only be made with pork. Any other meat would turn too dry.

It's a highly technical dish that demands both hard work and an understanding of organ meat, not to mention an ability to predict the future with some accuracy. The pork is thrice-cooked and traditionally served with *sanna* (steamed rice cake), bread or rice.

250

The process begins with rubbing the meat with salt and turmeric, both to clean it and to create an inhospitable environment for germs. The meat is then cut into manageable chunks and braised in water until just cooked through — no more. Once cooled, it's cut into ¼ inch cubes and seared in a hot pan to crisp up the rind. Finally, the cubes are poached in a masala paste to create the finished dish.

The masala itself is ground using only vinegar, never water, which makes it quite sharp at first hence the need to reheat it daily for a week to let the flavours balance out. *Sorpotel* is one of those rare dishes that improves with age, though it seldom lasts long enough to prove the point; it tends to disappear quickly.

Traditionally, *sorpotel* uses pork shoulder and liver, with each cube ideally containing rind, fat and meat. During frying, the meat dries out and loses most of its moisture, only to reabsorb it later from the rich gravy, a complex blend of sweet, sour, spicy and umami notes.

Now, for the controversial part: *sorpotel* is sometimes thickened with pig's blood, which also lends a touch of sweetness. This requires certain artistry, since the blood needs to be freshly drawn and uncoagulated. When blood is used, some refer to the dish as *cabidel* rather than *sorpotel*, a term I'd never heard until I met my wife (yet another example of the North-South Goa divide). The version made with blood is typically darker in colour, almost black.

Sorpotel (Traditional)

Specific Equipment:

Mixer grinder or food processor

Ingredients (serves 4-6):

For the blanching:

- 500 g Pork Shoulder or Belly with the skin on
- 100 g Liver (pork, goat or beef)
- 4 cups of Water (or enough to cover the pork and liver in the pot)
- 1 tsp Salt
- ¼ tsp Turmeric powder

For the spice paste:

- 3-4 Red Kashmiri Red Chillies
- 5-6 Dry Regular Red Chillies
- 1 tsp Cumin
- 1 tsp Black Peppercorns
- 6 cloves of Garlic
- 1 inch Ginger
- 3 whole Cloves
- 1 tsp Tamarind paste
- ¼ tsp Turmeric powder

- 1 inch Cinnamon stick
- ½ cup Vinegar (Coconut or Apple Cider)
- 2 Tbsp Coconut Jaggery

For the gravy:

- 2 Shallots (or one red onion), diced
- 1 Tbsp Oil (or rendered fat from frying the pork)
- Salt to taste
- Sugar to taste

Method:

Blanching:

1. Pour the water into a saucepan (the water should be sufficient to immerse all the meat and liver, once they're added).

2. Add the salt and turmeric, and bring to a boil over medium heat.

3. Once the water is at a rolling boil, insert the meat and liver in the water, and let it boil for about 10-15 minutes, until it's just cooked.

4. Pull out the meat and let it cool down to room temperature as fast as possible (use an ice bath if possible).

5. Discard the water.

6. Separate the liver and the meat.

7. Peel the membrane off the liver. This is a chewy, tough membrane that can make the eating experience unpleasant.

8. Cut the liver into ¼ inch cubes.

9. Cut the rest of the meat into ¼ inch cubes, ensuring each cube has some fat, meat and skin on it, whenever possible.

Frying:

1. Place a skillet over medium-high heat.

2. Add in the meat only; don't crowd the pan, each piece of meat should have contact with the pan. Fry in batches if your pan isn't large enough.

3. Let the meat brown on all sides, allowing the fat to render out. Reserve the rendered fat for later.

4. Once all the meat is browned, repeat the process with the liver.

5. Set the fried meat and liver aside to cool.

The spice paste:

1. Place all the spice paste ingredients into the mixer/grinder and blend until they form a smooth paste.

2. Add more vinegar if needed, but don't add water.

The final cook:

1. Place a medium saucepan over medium-high heat.

2. Pour some of the rendered pork fat or oil into the saucepan.

3. Add in the onions and sauté until they start to caramelize.

4. Add in the spice paste and stir constantly for a minute.

5. Add ½ to ¾ cup of water and stir to combine.

6. Let the liquid come to a rolling boil, and then add the meat and liver.

7. Lower the heat to low and let the contents in the saucepan simmer for about 10 minutes.

8. Taste the curry and adjust the seasoning by adding salt/sugar/chilli to your taste.

9. Remove from the heat and let it cool down before refrigerating.

10. The *sorpotel* can be eaten immediately, but it's recommended to let it mature for a week for a better taste.

If you plan to eat it later, store it in the fridge and follow the process described below every day (for up to a week):

a. Heat until it starts boiling.

b. Simmer for about 5 minutes.

c. Top up with water as and when required to adjust the thickness.

d. Let it cool before storing it back in the fridge.

Serve the *sorpotel* hot over *pulao, sanna* or with *pao*.

Sorpotel (My Contemporary Take)

My Contemporary Take on Sorpotel

I've changed the cooking method to make it taste similar, but have more texture. In my version, the pork belly is crisped up so that it gives you a bit of a crunch when eating.

Specific Equipment:

Mixer grinder or food processor

Ingredients (serves 4-6):

For the blanching:

- 500 g Pork Belly with the skin on, cut into three equal pieces
- 4 cups of Water, or enough to cover the pork belly in the pot
- 1 tsp Salt
- ¼ tsp Turmeric powder
- 1 tsp Cumin
- 1 tsp Black Peppercorns
- 6 cloves of Garlic
- 1 inch Ginger
- 3 whole Cloves
- 1 inch Cinnamon stick

For the spice paste:

- 3-4 Red Kashmiri Red Chillies
- 5-6 Dry Regular Red Chillies
- 1 tsp Tamarind paste
- ½ cup Vinegar (Coconut or Apple Cider)
- 2 Tbsp Coconut Jaggery
- The spices remaining after the blanching process

For the gravy:

- 2 Shallots (or one red onion), diced
- 1 Tbsp Oil (or rendered fat from frying the pork)
- Salt to taste
- Sugar to taste
- The blanching liquid

Method:

Blanching:

1. Liberally salt each cube of meat and rub it into the surface of the meat.

2. Rinse off the salt under cold running water and pat dry with a kitchen towel. Make sure all the salt is washed off.

3. Arrange the blocks of pork belly in a large pot and pour cold water until they're completely immersed.

4. Add all the blanching spices and bring to a boil over medium heat.

5. Once it comes to a rolling boil, remove the pieces of meat and cool them down as quickly as possible without exposing the meat to more water. You can place the meat in a ziplock bag or bowl and place it in an ice bath. Don't let the pork have direct contact with the water/ice.

6. Place the pork in an uncovered bowl in the fridge.

7. Strain the liquid that the pork was boiled in and keep it aside for making the gravy. Don't throw away the spices.

8. Transfer the leftover spices from the strainer into the mixer/grinder.

The spice paste:

1. Add the spice paste ingredients to the mixer/grinder and blend until they form a smooth paste.

2. Add more vinegar if needed; don't add water.

The gravy:

1. Heat the oil in a saucepan on medium-high heat.

2. Sauté the onions until they start to caramelize.

3. Add in the spice paste and stir constantly for a minute.

4. Add the blanching liquid and stir to combine.

5. Bring the gravy to a boil and then let it simmer until the desired consistency is reached.

6. Taste the curry and adjust the seasoning by adding salt/sugar/chilli to your taste.

Crisping up the pork belly:

1. Remove the pork belly from the fridge and score the skin deep enough that it just reaches the fat layer. The scores can be diamonds or flutes.

2. Preheat the oven to 200 degrees and place the pork belly in the oven for 15 minutes.

3. Place a skillet with 2 Tbsp of oil over high heat.

4. When the oil starts to shimmer (don't let it get hot enough to smoke), place the pork belly with skin side down into the hot pan. There will be spluttering, and the skin will start to bubble.

5. Once the skin has sufficiently bubbled up, remove the pork belly from the pan and place it on a plate, skin side up.

6. Pour the warmed gravy over the pork belly and serve with *pulao*, *sanna* or *pao*.

Notes:

- For the best flavour, make the gravy 3-4 days ahead, and heat it every day as you would heat a traditional *sorpotel*.

- The pork belly blocks can be left in the fridge for up to 5 days in an airtight box and uncovered 8 hours before cooking.

Bebinca

The queen of Goan desserts. Legend has it that this delicacy was invented by a nun named Bebiana in the 17th century. The story goes that the nuns of the time used egg whites to bleach their habits, which left them with an excess of egg yolks. So Sister Bebiana combined the egg yolks with sugar, flour and coconut milk to create a sticky, layered dessert that came to be known as *bebinca*.

Now, that's a great story, and there might be some truth to it, but I doubt it's entirely accurate. After spending time with Filipino friends, I discovered two desserts that are likely precursors to the Goan *bebinca*: one is called 'bibingka', and the other "sapin sapin". In the Philippines, 'bibingka' is a coconut and rice flour cake, while 'sapin-sapin' is a layered glutinous rice and coconut milk dessert that looks suspiciously like our Goan *bebinca*.

My theory is that a Spanish nun who had travelled through the Philippines encountered these desserts and mixed up the names. When she arrived in Goa, she tried recreating it. Since glutinous rice wasn't available, she turned to her European roots and used eggs and flour instead. As further evidence, I'll add this: I've never known of anyone anywhere who used egg whites to bleach anything. Eggshells, yes, but not egg whites.

Back to the *bebinca,* making this dessert is a long and painstaking process. The batter itself is easy enough, but you then have to bake it one layer at a time, until each layer solidifies and caramelizes. The short version has five layers, the standard seven, the expert fifteen, and the boss-level twenty-one. My grandmother always made the standard seven.

Unfortunately, we didn't have an oven at home. So my grandmother had two options:

Option 1 – Old school style: This method involved building a coal fire outdoors. A large vessel was used, with the baking pan placed inside it, and the whole setup positioned on the coals. After pouring in each layer of batter, the vessel would be covered, and more coals would be placed on top of the lid to create even heat from above and below. Each layer took between 5 to 15 minutes to cook, which meant a total cooking time of 50 minutes to 2 hours, including time spent greasing the pan and pouring each layer.

Option 2 - The bakery: During the Christmas season, the village baker allowed villagers to use his wood-fired oven for a small fee. Villagers would take their batter to the bakery, and the baker would help them bake it. This had to be done between the hours of 9 p.m. (after the last batch of bread was baked for the day) and 2 a.m. (before his next day's work began).

My grandmother always opted to bake her *bebinca* in the bakery. So there she'd be at 9 in the evening, walking in the dark, batter and ghee in hand. And once she got there, she'd have to wait with the other women for her turn to use the oven.

Two-tone Bebinca

Ingredients (makes a 1 kg cake):

- 5 + 5 Egg yolks
- 200 g White Sugar
- 200 g Coconut Jaggery (if unavailable, use brown sugar)
- 300 ml + 300 ml Coconut Milk (divided into two)
- 75 g + 75 g All-Purpose Flour
- ⅛ tsp + ⅛ tsp Nutmeg powder
- ⅛ tsp + ⅛ tsp Salt

- 1 cup Ghee or Unsalted Butter (about 12-15 Tbsp)

Method:

1. Preheat the oven to 350°F.

2. Line an 8 inch baking pan with parchment paper.

3. In a mixing bowl, whisk five egg yolks and the white sugar together until the sugar dissolves and the yolks become pale yellow.

4. Add 300 ml of coconut milk and whisk until combined.

5. Add 75 g all-purpose flour and combine until smooth.

6. Strain the batter through a sieve to remove any lumps.

7. Repeat steps 3-6 in another bowl using coconut jaggery/brown sugar instead of white sugar. Keep the two batters separate.

8. Pour about a third of the white sugar batter into the baking pan and place it in the oven for 10 minutes.

9. Check that the batter has solidified. If it hasn't, leave it for another five minutes or until set.

10. Pull out the baking pan and brush some ghee over the surface of the solidified batter.

11. Pour about a third of the coconut sugar batter into the baking pan (over the previous layer) and bake it for 10 minutes.

12. Check that the batter has solidified. If it hasn't, leave it for another five minutes or until set.

13. Repeat steps 8-12 alternating between white sugar and coconut sugar layers, until all the batter is used up. In all, you should get six distinct layers.

14. Let it cool before slicing and serving.

Feijoada

Feijoada

Ingredients (serves 8-10):

- 2 cups Dry Red Kidney Beans, soaked overnight (you can use any kind of beans, but red kidney beans are traditional)

- ½ tsp Cumin seeds (or ground cumin)

- 2 teaspoons Kashmiri Chilli Powder

- 1 large Onion, thinly sliced

- 2 large Tomatoes, diced
- 500 g Goan Sausages (if unavailable, use a spicy chorizo and add an extra 2 tsp of chilli powder or chilli flakes)
- Approximately 2 cups of Water, or as preferred
- Salt as needed
- 1 Thai Green Chilli, slit through the centre
- Coriander leaves for garnish

Method:

1. Take the skin/casing off the sausages and place the meat in a deep, heavy-bottomed pan over medium-low heat. Add a splash of water so that the sausages don't burn.

2. Once the sausages start releasing oil, add the spices and the onions.

3. Sauté until the onions start to caramelize.

4. Add the tomatoes and sauté until they soften.

5. Add the beans to the pot and pour water to cover them all.

6. Mix well and bring to a boil.

7. Cover and simmer on low heat until the beans are cooked to your liking (about 15 minutes to half an hour).

8. Add water to adjust the consistency, and season as needed.

9. Garnish with minced coriander leaves and serve over rice or with *pao*.

Caramel Custard/Pudding

Caramel Custard

This European dish gained popularity across much of Asia and South America. I've seen versions of it in many countries: from Turkey to the Philippines, and even Mexico, where it's called "flan". The spices may vary from place to place, but the base remains much the same. Known in French as Crème Caramel, it's similar to a Crème Brûlée, except that instead of the crunchy caramel on the top, it has a soft, glossy caramel layer. Many cooks find it quite technical and tricky to master, but in Goa, it's so common that I believe every Goan who cooks has perfected it.

Specific Equipment:

- Baking dish that can hold at least 4 cups of water (7 inch round)
- A larger baking dish that can fit the above baking dish inside, with room for some water between the two

Ingredients (serves 8-12):

- 4 Tbsp Water
- ⅔ + ⅔ Sugar
- 2 ¾ cups Milk
- 6 Eggs
- Pinch of Nutmeg
- Hot Water

Method:

1. Preheat the oven to 350°F.

2. Mix water with ¾ cup sugar in a heavy saucepan over medium heat.

3. Do not stir. Bring to a boil, reduce the heat to medium-low, and cook until the sugar and water form a caramel syrup.

4. Remove from heat and pour into a baking dish, coating the entire bottom of the baking dish.

5. In another saucepan, whisk milk, eggs, nutmeg and the remaining sugar together over low heat until the sugar has dissolved.

6. Stir continuously until the mixture is just warm.

7. Remove from heat immediately. Don't let it get hot.

8. Pour the mixture over the caramel syrup in the baking dish.

9. Cover the baking dish with aluminium foil.

10. Place it into a larger baking dish.

11. Pour hot water into the larger dish, making sure it reaches at least halfway up the sides of the inner dish.

12. Bake in the preheated oven until it sets (about 50 minutes).

13. Let it cool and then chill in the refrigerator.

14. To serve, turn the baking dish over a flat serving dish with a lip, so that the caramel is on top.

Christmas Sweets

Kulkuls and Kormolas

These are the most common Christmas sweets made in Goa. Every household makes them, and they're usually the first sweets prepared for the Christmas season. Traditionally, once the dough is rolled out, a small cross is shaped from it and fried first, while a prayer is said asking for blessings on the household during the festive season.

There are two forms or shapes of *kulkuls*:

- Ridged cylinder (looks like a worm-wheel gear)
- Tetrahedron shape with opposite sides missing

Some (including my wife) insist that the worm-wheel ones are called *kulkuls* and the others *kormolam*; in my family, though, we called both *kulkuls*.

Kulkul (Kormolam, if you ask my wife)

Although common, they are not a particularly popular sweet — perhaps because they're simple, and people don't put much effort when making them. My mother's *kulkuls*, however, were a hit. I never got her original recipe before she passed, but I tried to recreate it. It's not quite as good as hers, but it's pretty close.

Ingredients (makes plenty to share):

- 500 g Flour
- 150 g Semolina
- 100 g Butter softened
- 225 ml Orange Juice
- 200 g Sugar
- Oil for deep frying

Method:

1. In a mixing bowl, combine the flour, semolina and butter using your hands until you get a sand-like texture.

2. Add the sugar and orange juice and knead into a dough. The dough should be springy and should bounce back when poked.

3. Bring the oil to about 350°F on medium-high heat.

4. Roll out the dough into a 3 mm sheet and cut it into 2-inch squares.

5. *Kormola* **form:** Join the diagonally opposite corners of a square without letting the rest of the sheet stick together, and press and twist a little so that it holds. Take the other two corners and join them on the opposite end, in the same way, to get a sort of double-pyramid shape.

   Kulkul **form:** Place the square on the teeth of a clean comb. Press the dough slightly so that a little of it goes into the teeth of the comb. Roll the dough outwards to get a worm-like shape.

6. Drop the formed dough into the hot oil and fry until golden brown.

7. Remove and place on a cooling rack with a paper towel underneath to absorb the extra oil.

8. The *kulkuls* can be stored in an airtight jar for up to 3 months.

Neureos

Another staple in Goa during Christmas & Diwali. It's like a sweet 'empanada' filled with either a coconut or a sweetened mung bean filling.

Specific Equipment:

Spice grinder or food processor

Ingredients (makes plenty to share):

For the outer shell:

- 500 g All-Purpose Flour

- 2 Tbsp Ghee (or unsalted butter)

- 1 cup of Water

- ¼ tsp Salt

- Oil for deep frying

For the coconut filling:

- 1 cup Shredded Coconut
- ½ cup Water
- 500 g Sugar
- 2 Tbsp chopped Cashew Nuts
- 3 Tbsp Raisins
- 2 Tbsp Ghee (or unsalted butter)

For the mung bean filling:

- 1 cup Mung Beans
- 1 cup Sugar
- ¼ tsp Cardamom Powder

Method:

Coconut filling:

1. Place the sugar and water in a heavy-bottomed pan over low heat and stir constantly until it comes to a boil.

2. Add in the coconut, nuts, raisins and ghee, and stir until the water evaporates and you are left with a sticky mixture of coconut.

3. Set aside to cool.

Mung bean filling:

1. Grind the mung beans into a fine powder using a spice grinder.
2. Add the sugar and cardamom, and roast the mixture in a pan over a low heat.
3. Once toasty, set aside to cool.

The final cook:

1. Mix the flour, salt, ghee and water, and knead for about 15 minutes to form a soft dough.
2. Place the dough in a plastic bag and leave it to rest for half an hour.
3. Divide the dough into about 20 balls.
4. Roll each ball into a 4-6 inch circle.
5. Place a tablespoon (or more) of filling in the centre of a circle, and fold the dough over to form a half-moon.
6. Crimp the edges using a fork.
7. Repeat the process for all the balls, making some using the coconut filling and some with the mung bean filling.
8. Heat oil in a deep pot until it reaches a temperature of about 350°F.
9. Drop the *neureos* gently into the hot oil (don't crowd the pot) and fry until golden brown.
10. Remove and place on a cooling rack with a kitchen towel underneath to absorb the extra oil.

11. The *neuros* can be stored in an airtight jar for up to a month.

Bolinhas

These are a cross between a cake and a cookie/biscuit. Although they are available at any time of the year as a tea-time snack, they are most popular at Christmas.

Specific Equipment:

Mixer grinder or food processor

Ingredients (approximately 1½ kg):

- 500 g Semolina
- 500 g Sugar
- 6 Egg Yolks
- 500 g Fresh Grated Coconut
- ½ cup Water

Method:

1. Grind the coconut in the grinder/food processor to achieve a paste-like consistency.

2. Mix the sugar and water in a saucepan on medium heat until the sugar completely dissolves.

3. Add in the coconut paste and stir well to incorporate.

4. Cook the mixture for 2 minutes and then set it aside to cool.

5. Once cool, add the egg yolks and mix them in.

6. Add the semolina and mix to form a thick sticky dough.

7. Preheat the oven to 350°F.

8. Line a baking tray with parchment paper.

9. Scoop about 2 Tbsp of the mixture and roll lightly between wet palms to form a kind of ball.

10. Place each ball on the sheet about 2 inches apart.

11. Repeat steps 9 and 10 until you have no dough remaining.

12. Using a skewer parallel to the baking tray, press lightly into each ball 3 to 6 times in whatever pattern you want. This will flatten the balls a little and create a design on the top.

13. Place the baking tray in the oven and bake for about half an hour or until they are golden brown.

14. Cool on a wire rack and serve as biscuits/cookies.

Plum Cake

While not a traditional Goan sweet, it has become so synonymous with Christmas today that many refer to it as a "Goan Christmas Cake". In most of Goa, the Christmas cake is a fruit cake, which is dark brown (almost black) in colour, and it's made with brandy and caramelized sugar to give it that dark colour and rich taste. My Grandmother didn't make Christmas cake; she made the local *baath/batica* instead. But my mother was from Calcutta (now known as Kolkata), and always made a Christmas cake the way it was done there.

In Kolkata, the cake-making process was very different from Goa. They'd soak the fruits in alcohol for over a month (usually starting sometime in October) to create a kind of 'rumtopf'. These fruits were then incorporated into the cake batter and were baked to make the Christmas cake. I'm not familiar with all the traditions, but I do know that the cake mixers would come to the house to mix the cake batter by hand!

The one Christmas in Kolkata that I remember, my mom had her sister call the cake mixer to come over so that my cousins and I could watch the process. At that time, I wasn't very interested, nor impressed with the cake mixer, but in retrospect, I have awe and admiration for the hard work those guys put in for very little money.

On a side note, I always found Kolkata to be a place where people were exploited. A key example is *rickshaw* pullers, who are still found in the city. A *rickshaw* is a kind of cart that can seat two or three people (like a carriage) but is pulled by a human being. Even as a young child, I remember feeling incredibly guilty (though not guilty enough to do anything about it) every time we sat in one of those.

Back to the cake mixers: these people would go house to house with their large mixing bowls. The homeowner would give them the cake ingredients. They would sit on the floor and, using their hands (no whisks, ladles or any other implements), they would cream the eggs and sugar and incorporate all the other ingredients, beating them with their open palms until a batter was formed, all the while being watched suspiciously by the lady of the house, lest they try and steal any ingredients.

Goan Christmas Cake

Ingredients (2 kg):

- 250 g Butter
- 360 g + 60 g Sugar
- 10 Eggs
- 750 g Mixed Dry Fruits
- 360 g All-Purpose Flour
- 200 ml Brandy
- Juice of 1 Lime
- 1 Tbsp Baking Powder

Method:

1. Preheat the oven to 350°F.
2. Pour 60 g of sugar into a heavy-bottomed pan over low heat.
3. Do not stir the sugar, but let it melt.
4. Once it turns dark brown (almost a walnut colour), take it off the heat and set the caramel aside.

5. Mix the butter, sugar and cream in a mixing bowl using the paddle attachment.

6. Once the sugar is properly creamed with the butter, and while the mixer is running, add in one egg at a time until all the eggs are incorporated.

7. Add the flour, mixed fruit and baking powder and continue mixing.

8. Add the lime juice and brandy and mix again.

9. Add the caramel and continue to mix until it is homogeneous.

10. Pour the cake batter into a greased (or lined) cake tin and bake in the oven for about 2 hours or until a toothpick inserted into the middle of the cake comes out clean.

Baath/Batica

Ingredients (1 kg):

- 6 Eggs
- 500 g White Sugar
- 2 cups Fresh Grated Coconut, ground into a fine paste
- 125 g Unsalted Butter, melted
- 250 g Semolina
- ½ tsp Salt
- ½ tsp Cardamom powder
- ¼ tsp Nutmeg powder

- ½ Tbsp Baking Soda

Method:

1. Cream the sugar and eggs in a mixing bowl using the paddle attachment.

2. Add in the semolina and mix to combine.

3. Mix in the spices, salt, and butter.

4. Cover and place in the fridge for about an hour to overnight, to let the semolina absorb the liquid.

5. Preheat the oven to 350°F.

6. Add the baking soda to the batter and mix to combine.

7. Line a baking tin (9x12 inch) with parchment paper and pour the batter into the tin.

8. Bake in the oven for about 30 minutes or until a toothpick inserted into the middle of the cake comes out clean.

My Mom's Christmas Cake

Ingredients (2 kg):

- 700 g Mixed Dry Fruits (the candied mix works as well), soaked in rum for about 60-90 days

- 500 g Butter

- 500 g Brown Sugar

- 4 Eggs

- 2-3 Tbsp Mixed Chopped Nuts
- 250 g All-Purpose Flour

Method:

1. Preheat the oven to 300°F.

2. Cream the sugar and butter in a mixing bowl using the paddle attachment until well combined.

3. While the mixer is still running, add an egg.

4. Once the egg is fully incorporated, add about 4 Tbsp of flour.

5. Keep alternating between an egg and 4 Tbsp of flour until both are used up.

6. Stop the mixer and fold in the fruits and nuts. Optionally, add about 60 ml of the rum used to soak the fruits.

7. Pour the batter into a lined baking tray (9x12) and bake for about 3 hours or until a toothpick inserted into the centre comes out clean.

Chapter 16:
The Big Fat Goan Wedding

The epitome of celebration in most cultures is a wedding. It is an event that offers the most in-depth insight into the cultural beliefs and practices of any ethnicity. Indian weddings are known to be a grand affair, celebrated over several days. The revelry, traditions and ceremonies are virtually unmatched by any other. The Goan Catholic wedding is no exception. While in most Western countries, a wedding has become more of a legal affair than a cultural or ceremonial one, Eastern weddings are steeped in tradition.

The Goan Catholic wedding is traditionally celebrated over five days. However, with growing work pressures and families scattered across the globe, this is quickly changing, most wedding celebrations today take place over three days or less.

The celebration includes a variety of events: some are long, elaborate ceremonies, while others are short, lively and fun. Depending on which part of Goa the couple hails from, there may be a few extra (or fewer) traditions, but for the most part, the main ones are covered below.

The first event is the making of the wedding *doce*, a coconut and chickpea sweet flavoured with spices and cooked over three to eight hours. This is usually done three days to a week before the wedding. The preparation of *doce* (pronounced "though-sh") takes place overnight and is led by the matriarch of the family, with the women of the household assisting.

The men's responsibility starts earlier in the day, peeling and breaking open the coconuts. The coconut, finely grated on the *adoli/adori* — is used to extract coconut milk, which forms the base of the *doce*. Some of this milk is also reserved for the *roce*, another ceremony altogether. Both families prepare their *doce* separately, and always in large quantities, enough to feed a few hundred people, often the entire village.

It's a tedious process involving the slow reduction of coconut, coconut milk, sugar and the chickpeas until the mixture reaches a dense cake-like consistency. The concoction must be stirred continuously over an open fire for up to eight hours, depending on the quantity. It is then portioned and distributed to the wedding invitees.

Because the work is repetitive and exhausting, the women keep their spirits high by telling jokes and risqué stories, all in a sing-song rhythm set to the beat of the *dhol* or a *ghumot* (traditional Goan percussion instruments). The songs often have a chorus that everyone joins in on after each verse or joke. It's quite an impressive scene, lively and completely unrehearsed. One of the popular choruses I've heard goes:

Aiee go aiee go aikata muh go? Kazar jaishnu fudem mhaka kityak sangun na go? Vho cheddo, mhojo gho, mhaka traas karta kitle, poilee ratcher mhage chuddo tane phodle.

Though it sounds far better in Konkani, it roughly translates to:

"Oh mother, oh mother, listen to my cries. Oh mother, oh mother, why did you wait until the knot I tied? This boy, my husband, troubles me a lot. He broke my glass bangles on the very first night!"

(Artistic liberty taken to create the rhyme.)

Doce

Doce

Specific Equipment:

Mixer grinder or food processor

Ingredients (makes 1 kg):

- 250 g Split Yellow Peas
- 2 ½ cups Sugar
- 2 cups Fresh Grated Coconut
- 500 ml Water

Method:

1. Put the yellow split peas and water into a large heavy-bottomed pot over a medium heat and cook until they are soft and mushy.

2. Drain the peas and grind them into a paste using a blender.

3. Grind the coconut into a fine paste using the mixer/food processor.

4. Pour the ground peas, coconut and sugar into a large heavy-bottomed pot over a low heat.

5. Stir continuously. The mixture will start to bubble and splutter, but keep stirring until the paste leaves the sides of the pot and starts to come together into one cohesive ball.

6. Take the mixture off the heat and spread it on a greased pan to form a ¼-½ inch thick slab.

7. Let the *doce* cool and then cut it into squares or diamonds.

That brings us to the next ceremony called the *chuddo*.

The *chuddo* refers to the glass bangles — usually red or green or both — that adorn the new bride's hands. There are typically seven on each wrist, with a few gold ones breaking the continuity. Traditionally, the bride's maternal uncle (*mama* in Konkani) buys them for her, though any close relative may take on that role. The bangles are worn until they all break naturally and are one of the visible symbols of a recently married woman. It is said to bring good fortune to the couple if the *chuddos* break during the consummation of the marriage.

Now, if you go back and read that chorus again, it takes on a much more mischievous meaning.

The *mellya jevan* (translates to "dead's meal"), also known as *bhikra jevan* (meal for the poor) or *bui jevan,* is another tradition observed separately by both families. This usually takes place the day before the wedding and involves offering food to the poor in remembrance of deceased family members and ancestors.

The meal is simple: rice, fish curry, fried fish, crispy *papad* (papadam), and pickle. If the family is feeling generous, a serving of chicken, pork or beef is added. This meal is served to the poor of the village who eat it off banana leaves, while sitting cross-legged on the floor. Each dish is ladled out of large buckets by family members or, more commonly today, hired help. This ritual is performed to seek the blessings of both the ancestors and the poor for the couple's union.

The *roce* is the next ceremony, which traditionally served as a kind of beauty ritual for the bride and groom in particular, and for the rest of the wedding party in general. It takes place separately at each of the two homes, usually on the night before the wedding. During this ceremony, the bride and groom are bathed in coconut milk (*roce* in Konkani), which is believed to improve complexion and remove blemishes.

These days, with modern beauty products taking over, the *roce* has evolved into more of a "wet and wild" pre-wedding party. It usually begins in the traditional way: the bride and her bridesmaids (or groom and his groomsmen) sit in a row in their skivvies, while family members – starting with the eldest, bless them and pour small amounts of the coconut milk over them, making sure some lands on the face, hands, and legs.

As the evening progresses, however, things get rowdier. Friends and younger family members get in on the action, and the coconut milk soon gives way to all sorts of other liquids, eggs, beer, soda, and whatever else they can get their hands on (the grosser, the better). It's all good fun and often turns into a full-blown liquid fight that leaves everyone drenched and laughing.

The day of the wedding is a whirlwind, packed with ceremonies and traditions, and the constant criss-crossing of the family members between tasks.

The morning begins like any other, though the house is likely overflowing with relatives from out of town. It's chaos: queues for bathrooms, decorations scattered everywhere, nuptial booklets, favours, and boutonniéres lying around. Everyone has a job to do, while the kids are left to their own devices, at least for the morning.

After breakfast, the bridal entourage typically arrives. Most weddings take place in the evening, but preparations start early. Hair and makeup professionals bustle about, working on the bride, her entourage, and the other women of the family. The photographers and videographers arrive to capture every detail, the dress, the bride getting ready, and the preparations. A Goan Catholic wedding album is no small feat.

By early afternoon, the trousseau is sent to the groom's house. Traditionally, this was the dowry paid by the bride's family, but since dowries have fallen out of practice, the trousseau now consists of the bride's personal belongings —clothes, linen, sometimes a cupboard or dresser – along with some fruits and food.

In the past, labourers carried the trousseau in a small procession from the bride's house to the groom's, but with couples now hailing from villages and towns further apart, that has become impractical.

Around the same time, the groom's older brother's wife, or if he doesn't have one, any other older female relative, such as his maternal uncle's wife, takes the jewellery to the bride. This is typically the set that the bride will wear for the wedding, a gift from her mother-in-law. In some families, especially when the eldest son is getting married, the jewellery is an heirloom passed from mother-in-law to daughter-in-law.

By early to mid-afternoon, relatives disperse to handle their assigned duties: decorating the church and hall, coordinating with the florist, caterers, bakery, band, and other vendors – all to ensure the ceremony and reception go smoothly. With wedding planners now common, families have it a lot easier.

Once the bride (or groom) and entourage are ready, the photographer stages a quick photo shoot before the traditional family prayers. Everyone gathers before the home altar or, if you were among the elite, in the private chapel, to pray for a happy married life. Family members then approach the bride or groom one by one, blessing them and handing over envelopes of cash "to start them off." It's now time to head to church.

The wedding car is another Goan classic. Traditionally white, it's decorated with ribbons, flowers, and foam carvings, a symbol of prestige from the days when owning or even hiring a car was a luxury. In the early 80s, it was expensive to hire a car, and owning one was unheard of in middle-class families. So the couple (or more likely their parents) would splurge by hiring "a" car. The car would first pick up the groom and take him to the church, and then the bride.

When the groom and his entourage arrive, they wait inside the church. Only the best man, holding the bridal bouquet, stays outside to receive the bride. When she arrives, he greets her with the customary kiss on the cheek, hands her the bouquet, and escorts her (followed by her entourage) inside.

Unlike Western weddings, where the bride walks down the aisle with her father, Goan Catholic tradition has the couple, along with their families, gather at the entrance to be greeted by the celebrant and led down the aisle.

The typical procession order is:

- Ring bearer (often the youngest boy in either of the families).

- Flower girls, (who, depending on the church rules, may or may not sprinkle flowers/petals/confetti).

- The bride and groom, arm-in-arm.

- The maid of honour (holding the train) with the best man.

- The rest of the wedding entourage, in pairs.

- The parents.

Now, even though this is the Catholic Church, Goan priests make their own rules. These "rules" include: no sleeveless dresses, no photography inside the church other than a few with the priest after the service, vetting hymns selected for the service, and restrictions on decorations.

When my wife and I got married, even with a priest from the family officiating, it was a nightmare. We'd sent him the list of hymns about two months before the wedding and heard nothing back, so the choir went ahead and practised them. Then two days before the wedding, he told us to change to the hymns because they "weren't appropriate." On a side note, the church has mandatory pre-marriage classes, but let's not get into that. Suffice to say, if not for my family's religious beliefs, I would have opted out of a church wedding.

The nuptial mass lasts about an hour to an hour and a half, and is, frankly, the most boring part of the day.

After the mass, the celebration begins. Guests arrive at the "wedding hall" (the reception venue) before the couple, and help themselves at the open bar.

An emcee coordinates the events of the evening, backed by a live band (and more recently, a DJ too). The emcee decides when there's a big enough crowd to start the wedding march – tricky work since Goan weddings can have guest lists in the thousands. The idea is to fill the dance floor just enough for the march to look lively in photos and videos. Too many people, and the march gets dragged on for what feels like forever.

The wedding march is a grand welcome for the couple. It starts with the couple and their entourage circling the dance floor as guests shower them with confetti. Then the band strikes up a marching tune, and everyone pairs off behind them, forming a long conga-like line. The emcee guides the marching battalion of revellers into playful formations – the most popular being when couples join their hands to form a tunnel for the newly-weds to pass through. Guests occasionally trap them inside by lowering their hands and demanding they kiss before letting them continue. The march ends with the entourage at the centre of the dance floor, and the guests at the edges.

The emcee requests the two families to join the entourage for the cake-cutting, toast and the first dance. Later in the evening, the emcee announces the traditional father-daughter and mother-son dances, the bouquet toss, and the once-rare-in-Goa, but getting more common, garter throw.

The final tradition of the evening is separating the bride and groom, with the men forming a circle around the bride and the women around the groom. Guests take turns dancing with the bride/groom in the centre of their respective circle. The aim is to prevent the couple from reaching each other. The two are dragged across the dance floor with the circle of guests pulling them apart each time they almost reach each other. It ends when the bride and groom finally manage to meet and kiss — the cue for the night to end. Earlier, instead of the circles, the couple would be hoisted on chairs and paraded around, similar to the Jewish custom. But with tipsy revellers and one too many resulting falls, that practice has waned.

The wedding feast resembles a feast-day meal, but grander. It is almost always buffet-style, and while dishes like *pulao* and *sorpotel* are staples, certain dishes are synonymous with Goan weddings. Chief among them is fish mayonnaise, moulded into the shape of a fish, not symbolic (as far as I know), but an unmistakable Goan wedding icon.

Another must-have is *channa masala*, a curious addition considering Goa's own repertoire of chickpea dishes. You'll also find mussels baked with *recheado masala* served in their half shells, and crème caramel (or as we Goans call it, caramel pudding).

A now nearly extinct treat is *dedos de dama* — a lollipop-like confection with a hard, bitter caramel shell encasing a soft, chewy cashew centre, all on a stick. It wasn't popular, but I acquired a taste for it. It was typically presented on the buffet table as an edible center-piece, with the lollipops stuck into a squash or gourd to look like a bouquet.

Dedos de Dama

Ingredients (makes 18 skewers):

For the cashew marzipan:

- 1 cup Cashew Nuts, ground into a fine powder
- 1 cup Sugar
- ½ cup Fresh Grated Coconut, ground into a fine paste
- ¼ cup Water
- 18 Skewers

For the caramel:

- ½ cup Sugar
- ½ cup Water

Method:

Cashew marzipan:

1. Place a saucepan over medium heat and pour the sugar and water into it.

2. Bring the mixture to a boil and continue until the liquid becomes thick enough to form strings (when you dip a fork into the liquid and pull it out, it should have a string trailing from the fork).

3. Add in the cashew powder and coconut, and stir continuously until the mixture thickens and leaves the sides of the saucepan.

4. Take a small amount of the mixture, roll it into a ball, and place it in a bowl of cold water. It should retain its shape.

5. Take the marzipan off the heat and, while still warm, knead it into the consistency of a soft bread dough.

6. Divide the dough into 18 small balls and shape them into short cylinders with tapered ends (like a spindle).

7. Let the marzipan cool in the fridge for between one to six hours.

8. Insert the end tip of a skewer into the broader end of the marzipan.

Caramel coating:

1. Pour the sugar and water into a saucepan over medium heat.

2. Do not stir the mixture, but let it melt and turn brown.

3. Once it reaches a dark brown colour, take it off the heat and cool the base so that it stops cooking.

4. Dip the marzipan end of the skewer into the caramel to coat the marzipan completely, and leave to cool by sticking the skewers into a piece of styrofoam or a cake pop stand.

The event that concludes a Goan Catholic wedding is the *portonem*. It takes place the day after the wedding at the bride's parents' house. It's an opportunity for both extended families to mingle in a more relaxed and intimate setting while wishing the newly-weds a happy married life.

Traditionally, the bride wears a red *saddo* (sari) for this occasion, a remnant of the pre-conversion tradition where the bride (in Hindu weddings) is always dressed in red. In a typical male chauvinistic culture, though, there's no dress code for the groom.

During the wedding itself, family members are usually occupied with their assigned tasks and care of the guests. For the *portonem*, on the other hand, the groom's family has no responsibilities and gets some well-earned time off. The bride's family, as hosts, still shoulder responsibilities for the day.

Other wedding traditions are rarely observed any more. For example, the *saddo*, where the bride, mid-wedding reception, would change into a red saree (as is the tradition during a Hindu wedding ceremony). Today, however, the bride wears the red saree to the *portonem*, or chooses to forgo it altogether.

www.ingramcontent.com/pod-product-compliance
Lightning Source LLC
Chambersburg PA
CBHW061600120626
46550CB00004B/1566